Teacher Commentary on Student Papers

CONVENTIONS, BELIEFS, AND PRACTICES

Edited by Ode Ogede

BERGIN & GARVEY

Westport, Connecticut • London

Library of Congress Cataloging-in-Publication Data

Teacher commentary on student papers : conventions, beliefs, and practices / edited by Ode Ogede.

    p. cm.

    Includes bibliographical references and index.

    ISBN 0–89789–876–1 (alk. paper)

    1. College students—Rating of—United States—Case studies.   2. Report writing—Evaluation—Case studies.   3. School prose—Evaluation—Case studies.
I. Ogede, Ode.

    LB2368.T43   2002

    808′.042—dc21   2002025208

British Library Cataloguing in Publication Data is available.

Library of Congress Catalog Card Number: 2002025208
ISBN: 0–89789–876–1

First published in 2002

Bergin & Garvey, 88 Post Road West, Westport, CT 06881
An imprint of Greenwood Publishing Group, Inc.
www.greenwood.com

Printed in the United States of America

The paper used in this book complies with the Permanent Paper Standard issued by the National Information Standards Organization (Z39.48–1984).

10 9 8 7 6 5 4 3 2 1

Contents

Acknowledgments   vii

Chapter 1   Introduction: Some Words of Encouragement and Hope for the Teacher
Ode Ogede   1

Chapter 2   Comments in Context: How Students Use and Abuse Instructor Comments
Bonnie Beedles and Robert Samuels   11

Chapter 3   Overcoming Marginalization: Promoting Active Learning by Teaching the Technique and Theory of Margin Notes
David Strong   21

Chapter 4   The Teacher's Pet Phenomenon: From Dysfunction to Learning Model
David D. Perlmutter   29

Chapter 5   Teaching Generation X: A Dialogical Approach to Teacher Commentary
Robert Samuels   39

Chapter 6 A Shared Journey in Composition and Basic Writing
Classes: Another View of the Dialogical Approach to
Teacher Commentary on Student Assignments
Glenn Sheldon   49

Chapter 7 Writing and Relationship
Marilyn D. Button   57

Chapter 8 On the Margin of Discovery
Mary Theresa Hall   63

Chapter 9 Teacher Commentary: Put That Red Pen Down
for Now!
Louise Maynor and Sandra Vavra   71

Chapter 10 Rethinking Ways to Teach Young Writers: Response
and Evaluation in the Creative Writing Course
Stephanie Vanderslice   81

Chapter 11 From Commentary to Conference
Margaret Christian   89

Chapter 12 Moving Students beyond Defensiveness and Anxiety
in Writing Assignments
Thomas Earl Midgette   95

Chapter 13 Rigor, Rigor, Rigor, the Rigor of Death: A Dose of
Discipline Shot through Teacher Response to Student
Writing
Ode Ogede   103

Selected Bibliography   119

Index   125

About the Editor and Contributors   129

Acknowledgments

I am most grateful to all the authors who took time from their busy schedules of teaching and research to contribute to this book. My final debts are three: to Charles I. Schuster, who read a portion of the manuscript and provided useful feedback; to my wife Shianyisimi, whose love and friendship strengthens and carries me from day to day; and to Jane Garry, my editor at Bergin and Garvey, for her generous support without which working on this book would have been less pleasurable.

CHAPTER 1

Introduction: Some Words of Encouragement and Hope for the Teacher
Ode Ogede

This book has two goals: (1) to refocus attention on the overwhelming odds that literature and composition teachers face in American classrooms today, and (2) to provide some guidelines that can assist these teachers (and others aspiring to similar roles) in their efforts to set high standards and challenge their students to live up to their potentials. This volume has its origin in two separate (but essentially identical) teaching experiences I had in 1994 and 1995.

The first of these was an encounter with some of the nation's best-prepared students, in one of its most elite Ivy League universities. Very much in the tradition of the best research universities the world over, that institution boasted not only some of the most respected faculty in academia but also some of the most advanced networks of resources research money can buy in the form of vast specialty library holdings and very supportive, dedicated staff.

Having taught for several years in an institution of higher learning of comparable standing under the British educational system, it was, therefore, terribly shocking and distressing to be suddenly faced with a different set of student work habits, goals, and expectations. Not only were the cheers that are part of the acclaim a university teacher can typically hope for when he or she gives an erudite scholarly presentation in a British-style university lecture hall out of the question here, but, I could not understand why my Ivy League students looked with disdain upon the "top-down" structure of instruction and preferred instead a discussion format that allowed them to "participate" as "actively" as the teacher, in what they styled "a give-and-take" mode, which I found to be rather a trivialized affair.

I recognized that a teacher's ability to elicit student response could legitimately serve as a litmus test to measure what has come to be termed "teaching effectiveness." However, my Ivy League students' interests lay anywhere except in how I was performing my role as a teacher. Instead, the students were evidently far more interested in gaining control of the classroom space, which explained why they made a habit of turning feedback into an opportunity for engaging in self-indulgent and directionless self-performativity.

Whether it was because they did not feel I, as an instructor, had anything new to say to them—perhaps their acceptance in the Ivy League meant they had reached their intellectual peak—or whether their sensibilities drew them elsewhere, I found the mindset from which their response to teacher commentary sprang extremely overweening. All efforts failed to engage the students, the majority of whom continued to resist being turned into a captive audience well disposed to learning new things.

As I came to find out, the Ivy League is a setting in which the worst forms of ignorance thrive side by side with the most sophisticated forms of intellectual inquiry. Not only were the majority of the students that I came across here totally unwilling to assimilate any fresh body of information capable of destabilizing ideas they had grown accustomed to, but in my estimation, the quality of much of their classroom discussions left a lot to be desired as it mostly gravitated toward platitudes and was bereft of anything resembling the kind of lively conversation that is the result of attentive listening and profound learning. In short, what many of my Ivy League students thought they knew and wanted the world to know they knew lacked much intellectual depth, insight, and rigor.[1]

The apathy and tedium as well as resignation and chaos that stared me in the face in the Ivy League classroom stood in marked contrast to the venerable atmosphere that typified my British-style university lecture hall, where I could recall having always met students eager to drink from the fountain of knowledge dispensed by the teacher from his or her well-prepared lecture notes as these were delivered from the lonely heights of the lecturer's podium.

The second experience occurred while I taught predominantly minority students in one of the nation's historically black institutions of higher education. Though located only a few miles from the luxurious Ivy League campus, the small liberal arts black college, by contrast, had no comparable elaborate resources to aid learning. Not only were the shelves of its modest library taken up by antiquated books that were yet to be computerized, but, with all due respect, the greater part of its faculty did not appear to be among the most stellar.[2] Although even less engaged than their Ivy League counterparts, the students in this small black college were just as hungry for top grades.[3]

As I began to reflect on the sad spectacle of the American classroom, there was increasing evidence around the country to suggest that what I was observing was not an isolated occurrence. Though casual observers might not understand the troubling situation, and thus they might be mistakenly tempted to dismiss it as a shuddering happenstance, concerned individuals (particularly immigrant teachers from other countries) cannot but see an important connection between the students' post-teenage revolt and the wider decay in the national culture, all of which casts a negative light revealing a malaise of very alarming proportions.

Indeed, one need only to look at the country's recent history to immediately see a clear reflection of these kinds of behaviors in the world beyond the campus. As demonstrated in the irresponsibility of the Watergate scandal as well as the more recent Clinton/Monica Lewinsky impropriety, politicians' erosion of the bedrock of ethical political conduct can have fatal consequencies for the frame of the nation's moral authority. As with public figures' personal political ambitions or individual libidinal urges, so also with immoderate dreams of academic laurels: there is the same destructive zeal when academic rules are allowed to give way to individual students' personal academic career ambitions.

So what can be done to change the shuddering consequence of a generation of a nation's students who are not particularly motivated to learn or to respect constituted academic rules? If the students' misconduct can be particularly viewed as constituting an event all the more a cause for concern, it is because a society's future is usually seen through the action of its young ones. Whereas the students I was exposed to expected grossly exaggerated grades for the assignments they turned in, as well as for the exams they wrote, they did not seem prepared to work for those grades, which is to say they did not appear to be especially keen to earn the top grades. As a result, their obsession with top grades could justifiably be viewed as bordering on suicidal rebellion against learning as an activity, an attitude capable in the long run of threatening the very survival of education if left unchecked.

To the extent that any aggressive questioning of the standards of academic excellence and of expertise is an assault on the bases of the authority of the teacher without which education will become a sham and, the teacher, at best, would be rendered into something of a huge joke, these students' lack of motivation, and the total disregard they showed toward ethical principles of academic conduct, constitute a potent force capable of precipitating a major crisis of confidence in the nation's entire educational system.

Therefore, to think properly about the disquieting realities to which I was bearing witness in such markedly contrasting educational settings, I realized at once that I needed to step back a moment and abandon the ideal notion of education that I hold and sound the views of other teachers across the nation on the sorts of situations that I was encountering. How were other teachers dealing with the kinds of problems I was confronting? What kinds of comments worked for them and which did not in reacting to student writing? Where did they usually apply these comments? These are the questions to which the contributors to this volume have attempted to respond.

Some of these concerns correspond squarely to the unruly situation Peter Sacks, in his book *Generation X Goes to College*, has already spoken about in an uncompromisingly candid manner. Quite evidently outraged by the types of scandalous attitudes that I was worrying about, Sacks begins his book by detailing the rude shock he encountered while first moving into teaching as "a young," "ambitious," and "shy" journalist. Then, appropriating an eagle-eyed precision in tracing a teacher's coming of age, Sacks takes the time also in his book to offer advice on the diplomacy and subtlety—or more precisely the opportunism—every teacher now needs to survive in today's American college classroom and within the entire American college institutional framework in general.

Generation X Goes to College offers a spirited and candid examination of the contemporary American college teaching experience and should be required reading for anyone who wants to find out about American college teaching but does not know how to, for it attends very closely to the classroom situation, taking care also to provide a comprehensive guide that deals with issues such as the tenure process, student hostility, and grade inflation. Sacks's account of the happenings during his first class day, in the opening part of his book, is particularly relevant to our context because of his inventory of behaviors many teachers continually encounter.

For example, Sacks reports that, while scanning the classroom and "the unaccustomed sights before" him, he saw "young women trying very hard to look like models in fashion magazines with their big hair and big lips," and "something" he had not seen before—"at least in the context of an intellectual endeavor":

Scattered mostly in the back and far side rows were young males with professional sports baseball caps, often worn backwards. Completing the uniform of these guys was usually a pair of baggy shorts, a team T-shirt, and an ample attitude. Slumped in their chairs, they stared at me with looks of disdain and boredom, as if to say, "Who in the hell cares where you worked, or what your experience is, or what you know? Say something to amuse me." (9)

Anyone who comes to teach in the United States after having taught in the British educational system (as I did) experiences an even greater shock. Whereas the teacher is respected—even revered—for having attained that status under the British structure of education, he is treated at best as no more than a compeer by the average American student who is so used to pressing the claims of democratic equality in other spheres of his or her life that he or she is unwilling to accept (or is even incapable of recognizing) teaching as a terrain in which the exercise of power is beyond the control of the student, the apprentice.[4]

As noted by the contributors to this volume, in relation to this issue of power, there is no other area in the American college or school classroom at the moment as potentially explosive as that of assessment of student papers or projects which is inevitably completed with a grade and the obligatory teacher commentary. As such, it is the one matter—more than any other—over which students and their instructor must either negotiate or else they are likely going to get into a catastrophic conflict. Significantly, none of the contributors to this collection has successfully abandoned grading entirely; instead, all continue to give it a central role in student assessment.

Regarding evaluation, Ohmer Milton once remarked that "grading—the assigning of this symbol—is used for making comparisons among students and for record keeping purposes—not for informing students of the details of their successes and failures" (102). Today, however, such a remark can no longer hold true, for gone are the days when the distinction between testing and grading was so clear-cut. In opposition to Milton's statement students seem to regard the grade and the accompanying teacher commentary as informing them of precisely only one thing: "the details of their successes and failures," which is why in times like these teaching is all the more hazardous an undertaking in America.

Today's American students have grown touchier on the matter of power in the classroom;[5] their anxiety is further heightened by increasing competition in education. Thus, in places such as the universities and colleges in which the contributors to this book are all based—and without question in many others across the nation—teachers bear one uniform burden: how to deal with the fact that a teacher's commentary seldom garners more than a passing glance from students, since for most students the grade has become the focal point. As long as the commentary a teacher drafts with the best intentions is more likely than not to be taken as a corrosive attack on the personality and competence of the student, teachers face an even more intense pressure returning a paper with a low passing, or an outright failing, grade.

How can teachers deal, on the one hand, with the instant excited joy that greets the award of an A grade and, on the other, the commotion, grief, and angry outbursts that the C (or a lower) grade constantly attracts? How then can teachers balance students' emotional needs with an obligation to give honest advice? How can teachers help students see the bitter truth without causing psychological trauma; be direct without being brutal, explicit without being wounding, critical without being intimidating? These are some of the questions addressed in this book, which is about helping literature and composition teachers find a way to deal with these difficulties.

Though none of the thirteen contributors to this volume would now endorse the bizarre, cynical gimmicks conventionally employed by teachers desperate to win tenure (such as playing down one's expertise and resorting to grade inflation in order to gain the favor of restive students), neither are they negligent of the enormous risks continual resistance may pose. However, instead of bowing cowardly to student pressure, the contributors to this book have expressed a common cause espousing strong faith in the power of teachers to hold out against forces inimical to standards of excellence and of scholarly rigor. One contributor—David Strong—even goes so far as to show how students can put the power to assign grades into their own hands. All the other authors agree that, for scholarly commentary to be helpful, it should be pointed, but because critique involves human feelings, it should, nonetheless, take cognizance of standards other than the purely academic.

Some of the contributors (Robert Samuels, Glenn Sheldon, Louise Maynor and Sandra Vavra, and Thomas Midgette) begin by openly acknowledging (and implicitly decrying) the main obstacles that stand in the way of effective teacher communication with students. By emphasizing, in particular, the institutional behaviors which force otherwise conscientious teachers to compromise their integrity, these contributors help not only to define but also analyze and reject those obstacles.

Teachers of today live and work in a time in which grade inflation is bitterly deplored—both by teachers and by other advocates for high quality in education across the nation—as being one of the major factors not only limiting the enforcement of educational standards, but also dimnishing the capacity of educational institutions to provide realistic useful assessments of the performances of both students and their teachers. Curiously enough, teachers have been left alone in the battlefield to fight, as well as to bear the brunt of, the fierce struggle to stem—if not to put an end entirely to—the pressure to award grades that do not tally with student performance.

Therefore, to say that today's teachers in America work in a context where there is growing urgency for them to receive every bit of encouragement and support from everyone to provide students with honest advice is an understatement. The fact that the issue of fair grading dominates the thoughts and discourse of teachers at all levels of education—from first grade through graduate school—proves that teachers do not wish to shift the responsibility to anyone else, but only need the goodwill and understanding of their own colleagues as well as of administrators and parents and the students to bring it about.

Acknowledging that teacher commentary requires more than clinical diagnoses of the strengths and weaknesses of student writing, the contributors to this book argue that it offers the opportunity of developing a new methodology of composition, of taking students' writing (both creative and critical or analytical) along different directions, and of leading students toward an understanding of the various possibilities that are open to them.

Teacher commentary is a means of going forward, of leading student writers to find the way back from distractive digressions, and may involve the irksomeness of critique as well as the delight of praise. An exploratory procedure, it can lead students to consider material they have overlooked as well to complete information they have developed insufficiently. As such, teacher commentary should involve the revelation of new ideas as well as assisting old ones to reach their fullest expression. Not surprisingly, the most profound teacher commentary seeks to be open-ended and to push students to bring about the full flowering of ideas that may or may not exist in their drafts. At best, then, teacher commentary issues from the confidence to build on what is merely of potential significance. So teacher response to student writing can achieve its ideal form only when it takes cognizance of standards other than the purely academic, such as student background, work context, as well as students' different needs.

As noted especially by Marilyn Button, Margaret Christian, and David Perlmutter, teacher response to student work is a complex activity requiring tact and great intelligence to deploy successfully—the more so because it is expressed not only in spoken or written form, but also in body language and other communication media. Because it is easy to dismiss that which one does not understand, David Strong, especially, has even gone as far as to suggest that students need to be taught the technique of teacher response to student writing so that they are more able to value and engage with it more fully.

In gathering together this diverse range of essays from different disciplinary perspectives, this book affirms one indisputable fact: that society may look up to both parents and teachers to work together in fostering the education of its members but systematic impartation of learning and its evaluation must remain the exclusive role of professional teachers.

The individual case studies appearing in print for the first time in this volume should therefore have substantial interest as they can open the door through which inexperienced teachers can make their entrance to become expert instructors. Indeed, if they have no other use, these vigorously argued essays should make all teachers look freshly at how they respond to their students' writing. Reading these essays is like moving toward a situational clinic, for they not only tell the teacher what to do to improve his or her students' writing, but how to do it.

The strength of this book lies in the collective power of the examples the essays adduce and the resonance of their compelling testimonies, all of which boils down to the following: (1) If students listen attentively to what their teachers say about their writing they stand a better chance of being able to improve it; (2) students' all-consuming hunger for top grades can prevent students from improving in areas where improvement that can fetch that all-important grade is needed; (3) teachers need to remember that what they say (and how they say it) to their students has the power to change lives permanently.

NOTES

1. In my classes on African literature, many of the students debated heatedly about the Africa that is a figment of their imagination—Africa of jungles, elephants and other wildlife, diseases, famine, violence, and wars, where people live in trees—while I tried unsuccessfully to give them a different picture. For example, with the exception of South Africa, far more violence was being committed and reported in any single day in any one city in the United States, say Philadelphia, than all of the violence committed in an entire year in any of the countries of Africa south of the Sahara. In vain I attempted to caution that students not use the isolated case of war-ravaged Rwanda as evidence of continentwide African strife. Nor was I able to sell to my students the idea that many African cities have hotels and houses that compare in terms of size, luxury, and beauty with hotels and houses to be found in some of the biggest and best cities in the United States.

2. Susan W. Ahern refers in a recent essay to students in this type of setting, without addressing the social disparities that may have given rise to their plights, as "challenging student body," the majority of whom "may be juggling families and jobs, struggling with short attention spans or learning disabilities" (22). It is time now to tackle also the issue of the now well-known near-criminal funding inequities among the environments in which students and teachers in these kinds of traditionally black educational institutions function and those in which their counterparts in white colleges and universities in America operate—an invidious distinction that is a commonplace reality to even those who may be only remotely familiar with the operation of education on this side of the Atlantic. To the extent that the contrasting situations that I described reflect those inequities, the origins of which need not be rehearsed here, I will say only this: The only way that the United States will get anywhere with its efforts to restore academic rigor and high standards, as well as with its aspiration to put an end to a kind of evaluative political correctness that is eroding education in the country, is to eradicate these institutionalized disparities completely.

3. These largely black minority students are unquestionably the victims of a self-perpetuating situation that enfeebles a group's sense of worth as human beings.

For, as a group, they live and work under conditions that inevitably give rise to low morale. Although crippled by lack of facilities, these black students' low performance (like that of the majority of their teachers, which is a spin off of a combination of low pay and of lack of great research facilities) often leads to their being eclipsed by their colleagues in more prestigious institutions, an eclipse that in turn perpetuates a continuing feeling of inadequacy that leaves both groups mired in the path of a low achievement pattern that further helps to confirm the way society has labeled them as intellectually incompetent.

4. Another striking feature of American life is the dominant power and influence exercised by the media and the entertainment industry. A situation, whereby, in the thrall of the media culture, television talk-show hosts exercise more muscle than university intellectuals in the formation and shaping of the nation's culture will no doubt evoke a feeling among foreign observers of American society of something akin to institutional endorsement of mediocrity or just plain stupidity. Indeed, this relative lack of recognition of the importance of education in the United States is further shown both by the general low funding for education and the fact that teachers are more specifically foremost among the group of workers shown the most evident lack of respect as demonstrated in the poor salaries and perks they are paid compared to other professionals—for example, NBA players who make millions of dollars annually despite some of them being semi-literate, whereas it is rare to find in this country a college professor who earns above the five digit figure. (This is not to deny, of course, that—to judge by the internal departmental squabbles, feuds, and other forms of wrangling succinctly described by Richard Wentz as "methodological ostracism, tenure reprisals, salary rebuffs, or other forms of political disdain" (B5) rife in the academy—professors are their own worst enemies.)

5. For a comprehensive discussion of one prominent approach to power sharing in the classroom, see Ira Schor (1996).

WORKS CITED

Ahern, Susan W. "Conducting a Successful Local Job Search." *Ade Bulletin* 129 (Fall 2001): 21–23.

Milton, Ohmer. *On College Teaching: A Guide to Contemporary Practices*. San Francisco: Jossey-Bass Publishers, 1978.

Sacks, Peter. *Generation X Goes to College: An Eye-Opening Account of Teaching in Postmodern America*. Chicago: Open House Court Press, 1996.

Schor, Ira. *When Students Have Power: Negotiating Authority in a Critical Pedagogy*. Chicago: University of Chicago Press, 1996.

Wentz, Richard E. "The Merits of Professors Emeriti." *The Chronicle of Higher Education*, 14 December 2001, B5.

CHAPTER 2

Comments in Context: How Students Use and Abuse Instructor Comments

Bonnie Beedles and Robert Samuels

Surrounded by a stack of student papers, most composition instructors have, no doubt, wondered whether there is any use in writing extensive comments, as they contemplate the overwhelming and time-consuming nature of such work. They may wonder how carefully students read comments; whether they read comments at all; how or whether comments on completed essay assignments serve any kind of instructional purpose; and even to what extent their comments—and which comments—actually help students revise their essays.

The issue of instructor comment effectiveness has been studied and debated among composition researchers for years. Much of this work has focused on the types of comments that are most effective, and some interesting—and conflicting—findings have been reported in this area. In order to extend this mode of analysis, several members (Bonnie Beedles, Pam Inglesby, Madeleine Sorapure, Patrick McHugh, and George Yatchisin) of the Writing Program at the University of California at Santa Barbara (UCSB) developed a pilot study centered on examining the diverse responses of students to teachers' commentaries. While this study is still being completed, we would like to discuss some of the preliminary results and pose several important questions about the limi-

understanding that they would subsequently revise the essays for a new grade. The instructors responded to the papers with the same kinds of written assignments they normally use when students are to revise a paper.[1] After the students had handed in their revised essays, we asked them to bring the original versions as well, and we had a researcher come into the class to describe the study and distribute the surveys to the students, whom we instructed to number all the comments written on their first drafts. Afterwards, we conducted a survey to ascertain which comments the students used for revising and asked several different types of questions to determine comment usefulness.

The questionnaires consisted of three segments. One part required the students to rate the extent to which they felt they used each comment in their revision, from a scale of 1–5; the other part sought to know whether or not the students discussed the written comments with their instructor, a tutor, or anyone else; and the last section asked them to note the three most and least useful comments and their reasons for so classifying these comments. We made copies of both the first and the revised drafts of the students' essays and assigned code letters to them as well as the questionnaires, linking all their three parts, distinguishing each student, and noting each student's instructor.

In analyzing our results, we used a coding sheet adapted from the focus, specificity, and mode categorizations delineated in Richard Straub and Ronald Lunsford's *Twelve Readers Reading* (160–83) as well as in Straub's 1997 study. We checked intercoder reliability among the four coders, starting with ten essays from a single instructor's class, and categorizing all the numbered comments appearing on the papers.[2]

Next, our procedure called for much more in-depth analysis than what we have described thus far. We checked our intercode reliability and then coded the comments of the remaining 126 essays, as we tried both to establish the qualitative patterns in the usefulness ratings assigned by students to particular comments and, even more ambitiously, to measure improvement from first to second drafts.

Although we knew the difficulty involved in measuring improvement, which can be a highly subjective enterprise, we believed we could do it to a certain degree of success. For example, we could tell whether or not a given student made any changes at all in response to the instructor's comments. Further, we could determine what kinds of categorization we could assign to the changes—be it at the levels of focus, or of specificity and mode. We also could note any patterns between the comment modes and the changes made—either within particular classroom populations or between all the Writing 1 students. While sticking to these quantitative definitions of improvement, we also held out hope that we could somehow extend our analysis to more explicitly address the quality of the changes made.

Our results for the first ten papers are instructive in the variety of data generated and their implications. Looking at the degree of intercoder reliability in the categorizations our four coders gave to the 285 total comments on the ten papers, our agreement rate was high: an 85 percentage agreement rate. We found that surface errors showed the marked improvement, partly because of the revisions elicited by the corrective/explanatory comments.[3] We also found that students generally used more specific and more directive comments simply because such comments require the least amount of effort for inexperienced student writers.

Throughout our study, we observed a strong correlation between the directness of a teacher's comments and a student's sense of the effectiveness of the comments. The following examples display the diverse ways that the students responded to the teachers' direct comments:

1. *Teacher's direct comment on content*: "Just because it is new doesn't make it sovereign—Percy says you can approach new things either as a sovereign person or as a sightseer/tourist." *Student's response*: "This was a useful comment because it helps my paper get started better. It was a bit confusing before."
2. *Teacher's direct comment on style*: "Introduce this quote more fully." *Student's response*: "This helps the reader understand the syntax of my quote."
3. *Teacher's open comment on form*: "I don't see how what you discuss next relates to what you just said." *Student's response*: "I found this comment useful because it caused me to revise my first paragraph, so everything could relate."
4. *Teacher's comment on word choice*: "Why do you say 'absorbed'? From what/where?" *Student's response*: "I wrote the sentence, 'I completed my last final for the fall quarter on Wednesday, and the feeling of relief I absorbed into my body was awesome.' I did not find the comment on this sentence useful because all I did was delete 'I absorbed into my body.' "

Most of the students may value direct comments that give them straightforward help in the revision process (which is one reason they gave high ratings to areas involving word choice, content, form, and style). Interestingly, there were instances where students incorporated the teacher's suggestions but still claimed that the same teacher's comment was not useful. Many such cases involved single word corrections or abbreviated signs. For instance, in response to a question mark that was placed above a word, a student wrote: "This was not useful because it showed that the teacher did not fully understand my paper." Since the teacher did not articulate the problem clearly, the student was able to blame the teacher for the lack of understanding. Yet another student expressed the view that a teacher's comment on word choice was not useful because it was too direct, stating that the comment was to replace "among" with "in"—a correction this particular student felt was too overtly direct to give him any freedom or choice in revision. For this student, direct comments regarding specific grammatical errors are, in fact, "insignificant" and "knitpicking [*sic*]."

It was statements that directly questioned the students' ideas that caused the vastest majority of negative reactions by students to the teachers' commentaries, however. For example, one student responded to a teacher's note asking her if the "author poses any solutions?" by stating that, "She [that is, the teacher] wanted me to add ideas that I believe had nothing to do with the topic. So I ignored her comment." There were many similar cases of active resistance to teacher commentary. Some of the students seemed to resent the teacher's effort to redirect their ideas. Asked to re-examine the conclusion of his paper, a student wrote that he did not think the teacher's comment had "much to do" with his paper. Students tended to react in such defensive manner if they believed the teacher had a desire to impose new meaning on the main argument of their papers.

One of the more surprising findings that we encountered regarding the students' responses to the teacher's comments surrounded the question of praise. Out of the 15 comments in the mode of praise, students rated only 3 as useful, and none were rated as the top three most useful. This low rating of praise may be connected to the fact that many of these comments did not directly ask the students to make any changes in the future. While praise may have some important psychological benefits, it is hard to determine what effect it has on the actual revision process. Our investigation inclines us to question the role that praise played in Straub's initial study. For the high rating that Straub's respondents gave to praise may be directly related to the fact that his study was asking students about comments they preferred, not about comments they used or found most effective for their revision process. In contrast to Straub's study, we asked students about their use of comments, and we found the opposite pattern. The only praising comments that were rated as "useful" were those that included elements of criticism.

We realize that any conclusions about comment efficacy based on the results of our early analysis are so limited by the large number of questions and variables working against the small sample size; therefore, we are going to focus on reporting some preliminary results. Indeed, instead of trying to suggest any conclusions about comment usefulness, we will use a few of these initial results to raise important problems and questions about the limits of quantitative research methodologies for studying complex composition students and complex teaching pedagogies. We found that issues regarding wording represented some of the best examples to illustrate the ways students use and abuse teachers' commentaries. First, the instructor whose ten students' papers and surveys we analyzed commented frequently on wording issues, with 87 (or 31%) out of a total of 285 comments focused on wording. Second, 35 (or 40%) of those 87 wording comments were framed in the mode of corrections; the other dominant mode for addressing wording issues was the closed question category, with 25 (or 29%) of comments framed in this mode. Third, wording issues were 63 times given the highest rating for usefulness by students, where one indicated that the student "changed something in [his or her] paper to respond to the comment," and the student believes the paper is better because of it. In other words, 72% of wording comments were given the highest usefulness rating by students. By contrast, when we actually looked at the changes made by students to comments addressing their wording, we found that while most wording comments were attended to by students, the quality of wording changes was only high when wording comments were framed as corrections, and in about a third of the cases of the closed question mode. So, while students did use these comments, they did not use them well unless they were essentially told what to do to make a change.

In Nina Ziv's 1984 case study of four students' reactions to and use of comments, Ziv found that at the macro level, specific corrections elicited the most direct sentential improvement in student drafts of the same assignments. Since Ziv's case study followed students' progress through several writing assignments, she was able to track the long-term effects of different comment types. While Ziv found that corrections at the sentence level led to the most direct improvement, students typically did not understand the rationale behind these surface corrections; therefore, later essays generally showed little or no improvement in these areas. On the other hand, in subsequent drafts of the same assignment, comments framed as "explicit cues" of criticism, advice, explanation, and closed questions that point out the kind of surface errors made but do not correct them, often led to less direct improvement than comments in the corrective mode. Ziv concluded that students' later work showed more improvement in areas where the teacher used "explicit cues" rather than corrective comments because "explicit cues" are more effective in helping students to figure out how to correct their errors (375).

Our findings on two drafts of one essay assignment do show clear-cut quantitative improvements regarding matters of wording and correction. Nonetheless, we were also inclined to believe that measuring use of comments employing this methodology has almost as many limitations as measuring preferences for types of comments, for neither clearly indicates any actual learning. Our findings supported the assumption that specific and directive comment modes would elicit the most change from one draft to another and also supported the idea that comments focused on surface issues would evidence most direct improvement. The minimal grade changes recorded by the instructor grading our pilot sample of student papers also confirmed that the students did not do enough large-scale revision to merit much grade improvement. However, without looking at the quality of the improvements, and without looking at subsequent student writing, we cannot truly measure usefulness in terms of learning. If we simply counted the number of actual changes made by the students and ignored their quality, making claims about the efficacy of certain comment modes would be easy. Our preliminary work on this study raises a lot of questions regarding the appropriate methodologies for research in composition. Both ours and Ziv's results on students' use of comments on their wording make clear that the quantity of usefulness does not tell nearly as much as the more difficult task of measuring the quality of changes inspired by teacher commentary, though quantitative analysis may appear to be much more appealing because it is far less time consuming.

From ethnographic studies of students and classroom practices to case studies such as Ziv's, to the controlled empirical variable testing in studies such as Straub's, and to the naturalistic empirical variable testing embarked on by our study, methodologies in composition research all share significant limitations in terms of generalizability and conclusiveness of their findings. As Carl Bereiter and Marlene Scardemalia (1984) point out, empirical variable testing of the sort we began with rarely settles issues; it only adds "further increments to our knowledge" about writing (9). It was for this reason that Straub was careful to acknowledge the modest goals of his 1997 "a-contextual" study as being only to uncover "provisional insights into how students seem to react to various kinds of comments" and to "provide a foundation for further studies" (100). To the other problems of this topic, we must add the following pointed out by Straub: the difficulty in pinning down "differences in teacher comments"; in determining how "one element of commentary, and not another, has affected students"; and in distinguishing "the effects of comments alone from the effects of the classroom context and the larger institutional setting" (96).

Indeed, much earlier in 1984, Kenneth J. Kantor had pointed to this absence of "a picture of the educational context" as being the most glaring thing lacking in many composition studies. Kantor specifically pointed to the darkness surrounding "the conditions under which students write; the methods and styles of teachers; the personalities, attitudes, and learning processes of students; and the many interactions among these variables" (72). Kantor, who presented composition teaching correctly as "a multidimensional phenomenon" requiring "a research methodology that will account for its complexity," went on to offer a forceful argument in favor of the uses of ethnographic and other approaches that could help researchers to "discover these varied aspects of how writing is taught and learned" (72).

The data generated from our pilot study and the dramatic contrasts between our quantitative and qualitative findings erode our faith in the efficacy of quantitative measures for drawing conclusions about student writing and instead offer support for the use of qualitative analysis currently enjoying a boom period in the field. Ultimately, we look forward to the time when composition teachers face less demanding teaching schedules so that they can focus on learning more about how students learn in the real context of writing classrooms. Only then can composition teachers know how to write comments that are not only based less upon tentative assumptions but also could serve as more effective teaching tools than their current practices.

NOTES

1. Although they were available (as usual) for student-initiated conferences to discuss their written assignments and revising strategies in general, during the revision exercises, the instructors did not require mandatory conferences with the students.

2. The calculations of inter-coder reliability are based on the simple premise that there were significant disagreements on only an average of 12 comments per student out of all 3 possible categorizations. Since the papers contained an average of 28 comments per paper for a total average of 84 categorizations per student, per paper, this works out to an 85% agreement rate. While about half of our disagreements concerned the specificity of comments, many of what we ended up counting as disagreements in comment focus or mode were really mixed combinations of comment types. With more time to run more sophisticated analyses, mixed comments could be separated from disagreements, resulting in lower disagreement rate.

3. Unfortunately many composition instructors would be familiar with getting supposedly revised papers back from students that merely show correction of all the sentence-level errors noted and that undertake little or none of the kinds of large-scale revisions that composition teachers typically value most highly.

WORKS CITED

Beach, R. "Self-Evaluation Strategies of Extensive Revisers and Non-Revisers." *College Composition and Communication* 27.2 (1976): 160–64.

Bereiter, C., and M. Scardemalia. "Levels of Inquiry in Writing Research." P. Mosenthal, L. Tamor, and S. A. Walmsley, ed. In *Research on Writing: Principles and Methods*, edited by 3–25. New York: Longman, 1984.

Burkland, J, and N. Grimm. "Motivating through Responding." *Journal of Teaching Writing* 5 (1986): 237–47.

Fuller, D. "Teacher Commentary That Communicates: Practicising What We Preach in the Writing Class." *Journal of Teaching Writing* 6 (Fall/Winter 1987): 307–17.

Hodges, E. "The Unheard Voices of Our Responses to Students' Writing." *Journal of Teaching Writing* 11 (1992): 203–18.

Horvath, B. "The Components of Written Response: A Practical Synthesis of Current Views." *Rhetoric Review* 2 (January 1984): 136–56.

Kantor, K.J. "Classroom Contexts and the Development of Writing Institutions: An Ethnographic Case Study." In *New Directions in Composition Research*, edited by R. Beach, and L.S. Bridwell, 72–94. New York: Guilford Press, 1984.

Knoblauch, C.H., and L. Brannon. "Responding to Texts: Facilitating Revision in the Writing Workshop." In *Rhetorical Traditions and the Teaching of Writing*, edited by C.H. Knoblauch and L. Brannon. Upper Montclair, NJ: Boynton/Cook, 1984. 118–50.

Lauer, J.M., and W.J. Asher. *Composition Research/Empirical Designs*. New York: Oxford University Press, 1988.

Moxley, J. "Teachers' Goals and Methods of Responding to Student Writing." *Composition Studies: Freshman English News* 20 (Spring 1992): 17–33.

Probst, R. "Transactional Theory and Response to Student Writing." In *Writing and Response: Theory, Practice, Research*, edited by Chris Anson, 68–79. Urbana: NCTE, 1989.

Straub, R. "Students' Reactions to Teacher Comments: An Exploratory Study." *Research in the Teaching of English* 31.1 (1997): 91–119.

Straub, R., and R.F. Lunsford. *Twelve Readers Reading: Responding to College Student Writing*. Cresskill, NJ: Hampton Press, 1995.

Ziv, N. "The Effect of Teacher Comments on the Writing of Four College Freshmen." In *New Directions in Composition Research*, edited by R. Beach, and L. S. Bridwell, New York: Guilford Press, 1984. 362–79.

CHAPTER 3

Overcoming Marginalization: Promoting Active Learning by Teaching the Technique and Theory of Margin Notes

David Strong

After spending much effort and time vigilantly commenting upon a student's paper and then handing it back to the student, the instructor invariably witnesses the cold truth of teaching college composition. The student bypasses the carefully crafted comments, flips to the last page, looks at the grade given, smiles or frowns at it, and then shoves the paper into a beat-up folder. No matter how much care and concern a teacher invests in marginal notations, students are reluctant, at best, to read these comments. Students need to give serious consideration to teachers' feedback so they can improve their writing endeavors. However, before discussing what comments to write and which comments work best on a student's composition, teachers must address the vital issue of how to make the students read these comments. In this chapter, I propose a method that not only ensures that students read these comments, but also teaches them how to assess the underlying value of these notations.

Much like a judge ruling in the courtroom, a teacher assigning a grade to a paper or project serves, in the eyes of the student, as a judge on the ultimate worth of the paper and its author. Consequently, students perceive little worth in reassessing the value of their work or the process involved in its creation once the grade has been given. Instead of arguing for the elimination of grades or cursing the necessary evil of grades, I contend that teachers should embrace the authority that a grade conveys and learn how to utilize its power for good. To accomplish this seemingly Herculean feat, instructors must teach the students how to assign grades and what criteria to use. By putting composition students in the position of grader and primary interpreter of what distinguishes effective from ineffective prose, they acquire a confidence in their critiquing ability and trust in the grading system as a means to point out ways to improve their writing.

In order to achieve this goal, I maintain students should be placed in two-person peer groups when reading drafts, and papers should be returned with comments but no grade. The peer groups enable the students to grasp first-hand the care teachers exercise when writing notes. They begin to see that marginal notations root out of an individual concern for each student. I believe that it is the duty of the teacher to stimulate his or her students' curiosity in such a way that reading the comments becomes just as significant as earning the grade.

It makes sense to hand the paper back with the comments while holding back the grade. By withholding the grade for the first fifteen minutes of class, the teacher compels the students to read carefully and heed all suggestions written on their papers. Students need to learn how to correlate marginal notations with the established grading system and to collaborate with the teacher in evaluating the written work. Before these practices can clarify the different dimensions of composition and promote a self-reflective awareness of the writing process in students, it first must become clear to teachers that students perceive the task of reading marginal notations as akin to having a cavity filled: Despite the advantages it potentially provides, its immediate value is fraught with tension and pain. Because students view compositions as reflections of their own intellectual abilities, their focus on and subsequent interpretation of a teacher's comments can become highly sensitive and significantly biased. It is to avoid any discomfort generated by these comments that students expend their energy trying "to figure out where the professor is coming from." By so doing, they distance themselves from the comments, lessening the personal impact conveyed. No matter how positive the comments may be, student defensiveness undermines the insight and the help these comments are intended to proffer. Teachers can offset these misgivings by addressing student fears head on by first explaining to students how teachers approach grading and how they compose their comments. An effort at honest communication will underscore a basic principle of composition: that writing improvement occurs most often as a collaborative enterprise. Once students grasp the essential wisdom of this truth, they can begin to modify their perception of critiquing papers as well as to explore the possibility of working with their classmates and teachers to perfect their writing. Only when they are emboldened by understanding the benefits to be derived from marginal notes can students respond to teachers' comments with open, inquisitive minds.

Peer criticism is a good means to apprise students of the positive role written responses can play in developing composition skills because it affords them the opportunity to assume the position of knowledge-giver. When students get valuable feedback on their work from fellow students, they realize that such notes are not the final dictum on the value of a work, but simply some of the directions to guide and explain rhetorical techniques. Further, they begin to envision how the comments come from individuals like themselves, who possess real ideas and emotions. With this recognition, students slowly but surely come to understand the skill behind discernible, considerate remarks in the paper's margins. This method deflects attention away from the position of the teacher as one founded upon authorial power to the dutiful care that requires extensive knowledge of the writing process and individual intellectual development.

Teachers need to appreciate their responsibility to guide and support students' writing endeavors. Though it may seem simplistic to point out, every normal student wants to better his or her writing experience. Teachers need constantly to appraise their own worth by resolving any confusion or queries stemming from marginal commentary. When the context of the comments is not clear to students, teachers must be willing to explain its import. A consistent interactive exchange has to be developed in order to create an environment of trust, curiosity, and creativity.

When students are made conscious that comments on their papers reflect the good intentions of actual persons who genuinely want to help them to improve their writing skills, students begin to express their ideas and responses in a mindful manner. Skeptics may be concerned that peer criticism only makes students aware of their classmate's writing level but rarely results in any constructive understanding of marginal notations. In certain scenarios such a claim is plausible; for example, when the teacher places the students into groups and simply makes a general announcement that the students should read each other's papers. Without any explanation or perceived sense of value, students will not respond critically or enthusiastically to such an assignment.

However, this type of unfortunate result can be clearly avoided if the teacher exercises a self-reflexive understanding of marginal notations and requires two specific tasks of students. First, ask the students to write one constructive piece of criticism and two positive comments upon the paper. The purpose of this mandate is apparent to those teachers who have tried peer criticism in their classes. Since students are afraid to make negative comments on one another's paper, a classwide requirement directing them to write a constructive piece of criticism places all the students in the same position. No longer do they have to fear hurting someone else's feelings or fear retribution from another student for critiquing his or her paper. The psychologically aware teacher utilizes an experiental knowledge of students' attitude toward marginal notations and transforms apprehension into a desire to learn and hone composition skills. Now, a student's "constructive piece of criticism" is not seen as a personal mark against a fellow classmate, but as an actual part of the course and as an area in genuine need of improvement.

Next, because of the students' inexperience, the teacher should draw strength from his or her own pedagogical expertise and urge the students to imitate the teacher's method of drafting responses. Advising students to follow the manner their papers have been commented upon sparks a real critical interest in the commentary writing process. Students become actively involved when they are encouraged to pull out and peruse their old papers to see what suggestions have been made and why. They certify for themselves the significance of the teacher's commentary, and they bond with the teacher. As the authoritarian barrier between teacher and student dissolves, students increase their analytical ability. The value of positive rapport—between students and the instructor as well as among the students—cannot be overemphasized.

It is wise to make students base their responses upon the teacher's more mature approach. One way in which people learn quickly and effectively is through example. Helping students evaluate written work by incorporating insights from their own experiences with what they learn from their teachers builds considerable belief in students' own abilities. It can alter students' misconceptions that marginal notes are arbitrary and bear no relation to the students' own scope of learning. It can build an openness to examine the value of those comments written on their papers, and it can promote discovery and discussion. It motivates students to freely discuss with one another how the comments their papers have attracted apply to those issues raised in their fellow students' papers.

Posing such questions as the following is essential to promoting critical exchange between students, and between the students and the instructor:

"Why? Explain your reasoning."
"Develop this idea more elaborately."
"Is this a logical connection to your previous point?"

Students can draw encouragement from the teacher to learn from and apply his or her comments in answering questions such as these. Notes raising queries that demand further explanation discourage students' becoming merely passive recipients in a learning situation. Instead of merely answering "yes" or "no," students become active learners, who exercise key thoughts and abilities to compose and revise written work.[1] Because they facilitate dialogue, questions can serve as key supplements to the directive a teacher gives students to improve their work. Enabling students to begin to talk about the writing concerns is a way to empower them. The sense of authority and expertise vitalizes students' writing experience and builds belief in themselves. Students' desire to help each other increases, as well as the recognition of the value of positive criticisms and the willingness to express their ideas clearly.

The teacher's passion for increasing students' interest in marginal notes should not be limited to theory alone. To guarantee effectiveness, practical peer criticism should not commence until the first paper has been handed back with the teacher's comments. This is necessary because students must first gain a concrete sense of the nature of comments. Students often consider grammar problems to be the main issue in composition classes. Not until they have recieved their first paper back are they able to see that the more substantive concerns may focus upon some other things such as explication, logic, and other rhetorical matters.

Ideally the first paper exemplifies the kinds of marginal notations acceptable in the class and establishes the expectations in the course. Obviously, since the first paper functions as a model for all subsequent papers, it does not carry much weight in the final grade tabulation. However, with the first paper in hand, students begin investing interest in the class, and when they have completed the assigned draft for the second paper, they can be placed into small groups. I usually put the students into two-person groups and if there is an odd number of students, I have one group of three students.

To imprint upon their minds the importance of the exercise, I place the students with those classmates whom they do not regularly sit next to. Under this arrangement, they are not so inclined to chat lightly during the time or gloss over the paper in fear of upsetting their close friend. In addition, they get to know other students in the class so that by the end of the semester, everyone, whether or not they sit next to each other, knows everyone else in class, and the discussions flow freely and actively. Urging them to master the skill of writing commentary, I stress that they should review the comments written on their graded papers and apply the criteria on those papers to the drafts they are reading. Sitting next to a new face and confronted with a meaningful responsibility, the students without fail critique the drafts with the seriousness the assignment deserves.

Indeed, as the semester progresses, I hear the students comment in their two-person groups, "You have to change this. You know the professor won't accept this generalization." The other student nods his or her head in agreement, and they both lean over and try to hammer out a sentence or expression as clearly as possible. I believe the students respond so enthusiastically not only because they feel placed in a position that obliges them to want to prove to their classmates, to the teacher, and themselves that they can perform such a task intelligently and maturely, but, more importantly, because they find the activity a rewarding learning tool. I give the students 15 minutes to work in these groups and then change the composition of the groups. With classes lasting 50 minutes, these groupings can change up to three times per class period. As the students consider the commentary writing more carefully, I make sure the comments written are legible and sensible. This collective emphasis on clarity and meaning creates a new-found repect for the activity of crafting marginal notes. While my efforts cultivate a means to access the students' will and intelligence, the students' commentary enables them to enter into a world they once saw as beyond them.

Experience has shown that when students realize that they possess an intellectual ability not dissimilar to the teacher's in areas such as evaluation and judgment, students feel a sense of power. However, in order to get them to this level, the teacher must find some way to annul the distracting influence of grades by initially passing papers back without the final grades indicated on them. The teacher needs to channel the energy students exert in worrying about the grade into an ardent desire to do it better. Instead of being dissuaded by the constant complaint of "What's my grade?" teachers can transform this earnest desire into something positive, something that will intensify student interest in the writing process. In this activity, teacher commentary is an important component.

There is no reason why teachers should fear turning back papers initially without the final grade written on them. It can serve as an effective way to re-institute and guarantee student involvement in assessment of their own work. At my university, when students ask the perpetual question "What grade did I get?" I answer: "The comments are on your paper. See if you can figure out the grade yourself." Naturally, when students have the opportunity to assess their own work in this way, their curiosity is piqued, and staid passivity is replaced by genuine concern to decipher the meaning of the comments. Teachers need to realize one thing: Students' quest for success and self-improvement will compel them to follow what the teacher instructs them to do; all teachers need to do is to spell out their priorities clearly. The students will read the comments if the teacher really wants them to.

I have said that teachers need to be prepared to explain and if need be even to defend how the comments they make apply to each situation at hand. The requirement of accuracy and directness, without which a teacher's commentary is valueless, is a test teachers must be prepared to tackle. The teacher's commentary can cement a class together, but it can also sow a seed of dissension among the students. Teachers, if worth their calling, must be prepared to explain in a precise and conscientious manner the relevance and accuracy of the comments they make on students' papers. Teachers must realize that there could be a reason for students to be defensive about these comments, but when they are explained readily by the teacher, a most gratifying outcome results: students pay close attention to the mistakes or strong points that have been outlined by the instructor about their writing. But, in order to stop students from dismissing the teacher's comments offhandedly, a situation of mutual respect between instructor and student must first be created. When students rapport appropriately with their teachers, they respond positively to the teachers' efforts to help them improve their work—including those suggestions for improvement contained in teacher commentary. Since the grade has already been determined, teachers can help channel students' grade anxiety to productive ends without compromising established standards of excellence.

I am proposing that students should have their grades and comments passed back to them on separate sheets of paper containing a solid idea of the quality of their work and the grade appropriated to it. Such a grading strategy can translate counterproductive emotions into positive and resourceful tools. To achieve the greatest effect with this pedagogical strategy, the teacher should come to class with two piles of papers. One pile should consist of student papers complete with marginal notes, the other, a neatly stacked set complete with final comments and grades printed up using the laser printer. (I usually choose an eloquent font like Garamond to impress upon the students the professionalism of these comments.)

The power of this arrangement is that it captures the students' attention immediately. The students' eyes focus on and follow the two stacks. Even if these are the first set of papers for that semester, because of my grading reputation, the students are well aware of what each pile contains. I start class with the daily assignment, paying little heed to the stacks. It is crucial for the students to be in an academic, readerly/writerly state of mind to heighten their critical sensibilities. Once this state has been attained, usually within the first 10 to 15 minutes, I pass back the first set of papers. Fighting the impulse to ask what grade they received, they pore over the comments in the paper's margin to determine this knowledge. If their eyes stay focused on the paper, and they read carefully what is written, then I know that the students are striving to learn and understand my observations. Early in the semester, some of the students who have a great deal of commentary in the margins work under the false belief that the grade is a foregone conclusion; they assume that a "D" grade has been assigned. When some discover that these extensive comments accompany a "B" or an "A," they necessarily modify their perception of what marginal notations signify. What I strive to communicate throughout to students is that these notations can point to ideas to ponder more fully as well as mark areas of improvement. This sharpened understanding of the role of commentary increases student participation as students start to see that their ideas are the essential commodity in both class discussions and successful papers.

"I have to learn how to write for this professor to do well in this class. . . . My other English professor liked my writing"—those words, which many teachers have endlessly heard from their students, express the illusion under which students live: That each teacher has his or her own subjective set of criteria. The sooner teachers can get their students to come to terms with the truth that, while certain emphases may vary, objective standards govern effective, clear writing, the sooner students can set aside their defensive strategies and respond positively to feedback. As a matter of fact, what students must realize is that no writer is fully a writer until he or she has demonstrated a keen ability to comment upon someone else's written work.

NOTE

1. Erika C. Lindemann writes, "Formative comments, the kind that support learning, praise what has worked well, demonstrate how or why something else didn't, and encourage students to try new strategies" (227).

WORK CITED

Lindemann, Erika C. *A Rhetoric for Writing Teachers*. Oxford: Oxford University Press, 1994.

CHAPTER 4

The Teacher's Pet Phenomenon:
From Dysfunction to Learning Model

David D. Perlmutter

The dark side of the favorite pupil or the teacher's pet phenomenon has been methodically explored in the literature of student-educator relationships and classroom dynamics. Rates as high as 90% of students surveyed say that they have observed favoritism at work in the classroom (Tal & Babad, 1989). Favoritism can be expressed in many ways, from praising one student above others to various nonverbal cues of like and dislike (Rickey & Rickey, 1978). Moreover, students commonly express concern with the degree of favoritism of their teachers, especially with how it affects the amount of teacher attention and grades (Weinstein 1989; Morgan et al., 1992). In one survey, college students rate favoritism in grading as the most unethical behavior that teachers could engage in (Keefe, 1982). Even when favoritism does not seem to affect grades, it can affect the climate of the classroom (Tal & Babad, 1990).

The goal of this chapter is to examine the subject of teacher's pet or favoritism, and its relationship to written commentary on student papers. First, I emphasize the importance of the idea of teacher's pet in the contemporary classroom: how it affects students' attitudes toward their teachers and schooling in general and thus also affects how teachers' comments on paper are received—from whether they are read at all to how they are perceived as either fair or unfair and worthy of follow-up through discussion or not. Second, I make a radical argument: Rather than viewing the teacher's pet as a dysfunction, teachers should glean the positive attributes of the "ideal" student-teacher relationship and apply them to their written and oral interaction with all students. Finally, I operationalize this argument by outlining when and how to make the lessons of teacher's pet work for teachers in written commentary on student papers.

When I taught my first class of undergraduates, I kept a log of which students came to see me during office hours (and by appointment) and for how long. Purely an informal amusement at first, the data metamorphosed into a project that continues to this day. I have noted several patterns about the length and quality of student-teacher interaction; one pattern surprises me particularly: The students who came to see me most often and for the longest time were almost always the ones that I liked the most. Written commentary on their papers, or the quality of the classroom experience, or both, seemed to entice them to show up for office hours and beyond. I considered this a pedagogical success. The students who spent the most time in my office were the ones to whom I gave the most personal attention. Not only were these the students whose learning experience I enriched the most, they were the students who gave me the most gratification as a teacher. The fertile dialog was the one aspect of modern teaching not far removed from the ancient Academy, where Plato cajoled his young men, and where, as Milton put it, "the Attic bird trilled her warbled note."

Underlying all my pedagogical assumptions then is that interaction with students through comments, e-mail, or other lexical forms of communication is only one dimension of the student-teacher relationship. It seems to me that platonic dialog, without the actual moralizing and cant of the Greek philosopher, evokes the ideal teacher-student relationship, one which definitely can improve teaching in the most significant way in the contemporary classroom that even in the most well-funded small liberal arts college simply still does not allow for courses to be taught with the desirable richness of communication.

Indeed, there are several reasons why it is important not to restrict the learning experience to commentary. For one thing, we don't know whether students are reading it, nor do we know how they are perceiving it. For another, teachers may not even know how students are acting on it. In any case, the metacommunication of written commentary (e.g., "I, teacher, have things to tell you that you find useful") may be more important than any particular comment. It is imperative that the teachers review the commentary in person to explain, justify, and help students to apply it to future work.

Assumptions like those I have expressed do not downgrade the importance of written commentary on student papers, they only help to put these comments in context of the wider learning experience. Written commentary cannot stand alone—Students won't let it. It must be the introduction to a dialog in the classroom and in the teacher's office, not an end in itself. While the well-pointed critique of a term paper or the *bon mot* in an e-mail reply gives us some satisfaction, I argue that only through personal interaction can the written comments have full meaning for the students.[1]

Favoritism is relevant to discussions of the topic of commentary on student papers for several reasons. First, the comments teachers give students are necessarily not wholly objective. Many factors influence what teachers say to students, what teachers write on student papers, and what marks students receive for an assignment. No matter what steps teachers take to reach objectivity, they will fail partly because almost all courses provide leeway for the instructor to make judgments about the quality of student work that are based on subjective estimates. In many courses at higher levels, especially those that involve student research papers, critical essays, book reports, or term papers and writing exercises, the scope of subjectivity increases. Therefore it is vital to ask if what feeling teachers have for students affects what they get from the courses, not only in comments and grades but in learning outcomes as well.

Second, student-teacher relationships do not have to range into the obviously socially destructive (e.g., sexual) to have a possible nefarious impact on the education system. Many studies have repeatedly shown that students are aware, for example, of favoritism among teachers, and often resent it and take it as an example of inequity in the classroom (Engelberg, 1988). It matters then if we like, don't like, or don't care about the class and the individual students even if grades are not affected; the perception of favoritism, or teacher's pets and teacher's banes, may be enough to degrade the learning atmosphere for all students. Perceived inequity demoralizes students and is thus unconducive to learning. Moreover, being labeled as a teacher's pet may in fact undermine a student's relationship with other students (Moulton et al., 1998).

Psychologically, as well, favoritism and its opposite present a challenge to teachers' satisfaction with teaching. On the one hand, most "good teaching" primers advocate avoiding favoritism (e.g., Guyton, 1995; Orange, 2000). Yet, all teachers will admit that while they might "love the kids," they love some more than others. The bright penny, the engaging, interesting, hardworking, and even the polite and chirpy student who gives the teacher the most positive responses to his or her work necessarily makes him or her feel best as a teacher (Brophy, 1983; Perlmutter, 2001). Indeed, teacher assessment of students is hardly ever fickle and random: teachers unavoidably have finite sets of criteria from which they draw to assess students' behavior, which affects their relationships with students and then affects in turn teacher evaluation, although not necessarily student grades in the course (Parr and Valerius, 1999).

Trying to cut such ties would be destructive both to teachers and to their "extraordinary" student progeny. Because the absence of such reciprocity may actually lead to teacher burnout (van Horn, Schaufeli and Enzmann, 1999), there is a sense in which favoritism of this type is functional: Do not most great achievers mention a special teacher who took an interest in them? Rather than being discouraged from creating such bonds, teachers should understand the costs and implications for them as well as for the rest of the classroom.

There is an administrative component to this issue rarely considered by teachers: In any educational institution, whether private or public, it is a ubiquitous code of the teaching profession to try not to discriminate for or against students for any reason, be it of their racial or ethnic characteristics. To paraphrase, teachers are paid to teach all students well, not just some. Therefore, "all" should include students teachers like as well as those they don't like. Adminstrators have, in effect, promised parents that their children will get an equal education. If teachers let it fester without employing its positive lessons, favoritism may violate this contract.

Indeed, in light of the increasing diversity of America's schools, it is all the more important that teachers increase their alertness and sensitivity to the issue of favoritism in the classroom and the grade book. The day when college teachers and their students in this country were basically of the same ethnicity and background is ending: Classrooms, especially at larger public institutions, are fast approaching United Nations' committees in look and sound. It is natural that some of the rules of favoritism may be racist or ethnocentric, since people tend to like those who are most like them, talk like them, or look like them. J. Baker (1999) writes that, from earliest childhood, "special" relationships with a teacher whom the students perceive as paying close attention to them can be great incentives to learning and achievement. A reverse phenomenon might also concurrently exist, a sort of model minority affection for certain groups.[2]

In sum, it is important for teachers, when considering what students think about what teachers say to them, to reflect on what teachers feel about students. Love, as well as indifference, dislike, and hate, are normal human emotions that cannot be turned on or off at will. Their place within a teacher's behavior, comments, and grading toward students, however, needs to be identified, categorized, and examined. The goal is not to eliminate the biases of favoritism and disfavor but to make sure that teachers do understand and apply the positive and functional elements within teacher's pet.

Teacher-pet relations are conducted between human beings with pre-existing cognitive, physiological, emotional, and personality-driven preferences and prejudices. Therefore, teachers need to take cognizance of the likelihood that individuals may tend to seek out similar partners for the relationships. For me, I am mindful of the fact that the student most likely to be a pet in my class is the student who might be called the bright penny. He or she is the one who tends to speak up in class (but not too much), who expresses lively interest in material, asks a relatively high number of pertinent questions and displays enterpreneurial energy and forethought about projects or studies.

This is the type of student Tal and Babad (1990) refer to as the "high expectancy" student, the one the teacher expects much from in terms of classroom performance and approval of the teacher's own teaching style and skills.[3] He or she is the student whom the teacher percieves as having a high expectancy of performance from the teacher. This is the top student, and it is he or she who gets the teacher's increased attention in terms of class time, extra-class time, and commentary on papers.

Visibly, the interaction between the teacher's pet and the instructor is generally of a higher quality; this is noticeable to other students. In this interaction, ego validation is involved: The teacher's pet gets more praise from the teacher—orally, kinesically, and in commentary on papers. As a result, the Teacher's Pet feels better about him- or herself. The situation may lead to career enhancement: The teacher's pet gets more support from the teacher in his or her advancement in education and career pursuits. Because the practice can negatively affect classroom morale, as Babad (1995) rightly notes, I think that one can argue the teacher should strive to apply the lessons of the teacher's pet phenomenon across board to all the students.

Nonetheless, the emphasis in action plans should fall on student effort, on the student's own consuming desire to learn. Teachers' sentimental concerns with equity alone can idealize, and it will not do for them to understand and desire to apply the positive elements of teacher's pet phenomenon to all students. Virtually every teacher's pet comes to see his or her teacher during office hours and at other times because the teacher has asked the teacher's pet to and he or she expects a positive interchange from the personal meeting. An underlying assumption shared both by teacher and the teacher's pet is that the teacher's oral comments include points of interest on which the teacher's pet wishes to further follow up, and the Teacher's pet sees value (grade raising, career enhancement, ego-gratification, richer learning) in further personalization of the learning experience.

Certainly, all these entry points to follow are, it should be underscored, positive ones: Undoubtedly a teacher's pet might want to learn what he or she "did wrong" as much as what he or she "did right," but it would be the rarest students (or indeed professors) who want to face an aloof being who does nothing but detail shortcomings. Furthermore, within the interaction dialog of notes on paper or discussion in the office, suggestions for improvement can be placed within a positive context. Even if a negative critique may be the result, a positive point of entry for teacher commentary obviously offers a better opportunity for inducing clarifications in student papers.

Thus, the "please see me" note, for example, must be written with caution. As research has shown, students judge the note based on the degree of the security of their attachment with the teacher and the learning institution (Perrine, 1999). The marginal learner, the at-risk group member, may perceive those three bare words as a hostile introduction to confrontation (Baker, 1999). That is why I advocate not writing "please see me" in so many words. Rather, I suggest taking specific points of interest in a student paper—positive ones—as special gateways to further dialog. For example, finding a single statement in a paper that might (legitimately) prompt: "This is interesting—I hadn't thought of that. Can we talk about it some time?" Note that this does not mean that at the meeting itself shortcomings with students' work might not be introduced and dissected, but that the bridge of perceptual understanding should be based on a positive note. In addition, the notation should be sincere, albeit this may take some effort on the teacher's part for certain students' papers.

On term papers or writing assignments, I use a number of tactical maneuvers, either together or separately. First, as an introduction to dialog, I write the "please see me," within the venue of a standard meeting, not a special invitation to doom. I attempt requiring (or giving an incentive with "give-back" points) every student to see the teacher after each exam or paper. Office sessions can be scheduled ahead of time.

Second, what I call *negative overload* is a disincentive for students to learn what they are doing wrong and indeed to understand that they are committing any errors in the first place. Negative overload is in some respects gratifying to the teacher: we fulfill our "Kingsfield" stereotype of the "tough" teacher castigating the slackers. But again, the question is, what is the outcome? (No suggestions that I have made here calls for lowering of standards or inflating grades.) Simply put: the more the red, the less it's read. Too many (critical) red marks convince most students that their case is hopeless and that further communication about how to improve is pointless. To use a sports metaphor: People will overcome a hurdle, but will walk away from a stone wall.

That's why I suggest another tactic which, although it slightly increases the teacher's workload, better lends itself to student learning. In practice, what to do is to only hand back the first page of the paper. Keep the rest of the paper in your office ready to pull out for the meeting. This first page is one that you can mark—judiciously—but save your real narrative criticisms for the rest of the document. One way to cut down on red marks is to point out the first grammatical error of a type and then leave unmarked all repetitions of the error. (This also allows for students to make corrections themselves either in the office meeting or as part of an extra-credit assignment.)

Finally, a tactic to engage students individually is to return papers without grades—for these they must come to your office.

All of these tactical maneuvers allow the teacher to push toward that office meeting. There, the teacher can, as will be expressed shortly, personalize his or her commentary to each individual student.

Teachers may expand the lessons of the teacher's pet to the actual commentary on the students' papers. Certainly, as said, reducing negative criticism to single instances will help. However, beyond that the teacher must, as a Norwegian saying goes, "include some sweet to get the child to eat the salt." In simplistic application this means finding something good in every paper (and every student). But since at the high school or college level this can draw dangerously close to ritual (insincere) praise that only invites the contempt of the student, the teacher must see to it that self-esteem is built on stone, not sand.

I think a second lesson from the Teacher's Pet that can be applied on a more sophisticated level should deal with the lure of career outcome assistance. One of the characteristics that teachers appreciate and should encourage in students is the long view, the ability to see connections between classroom knowledge and life success. Note that this should not be confused with the entirely different mindset of the "show me the money" student. In my experience, enabling students to grasp that distinction is the hardest task a teacher faces. An example from one of my classes will explain this.

In a class in mass communication theory that I teach, most of the master's students do not wish to continue on to get a Ph.D. They thus enter the course, which is required of graduate students in our school, with some fear of and a general disdain for "high falutin' theory." Part of my job is to convince these types of students that theory is part of all life and work experience. Visionary leaders, for example, develop theories that allow them to succeed in politics, war, business, and so on. Therefore, understanding how to create, review literature on, critique, and test theories is part of all successful communication and professional employment even if the workers may not call it so by name.

The majority of the professionally oriented MA students resist this "lesson." Because only a few grasp my "theory is ubiquitous" paradigm, and even fewer begin to develop examples from their own lives that can fit into it, the challenge for me becomes to discover for the student majority examples in their present work and aspired career goals that can serve as "eureka" moments for each of them. The eventual use of teacher commentary as a prompt to open up such linkages for the students is what I advocate.

Typically, classroom discussion—right from the first class day—will elicit the students' self-reports about what they want out of school and their career. I have them write a short essay on the following topic: If, upon graduation, I could make a phone call and get you any job in the world, what would it be and why do you want it? Almost always students (graduate students) take this question seriously. They do not list silly fantasies but real entry-level career starting jobs. I keep track of these and find ways to insert what might be called *personal enhancement prompts* into paper comments. For instance, if a student wants to work as a manager for bands in the music industry, I tailor comments to known research on marketing of popular music: audience targeting and segmentation, demographic and psychographics, predictive patterns and models. These prompts are targeted by comments, such as "I want to talk about this. Could you come by for a chat?" I prepare follow-up information for the personalized discussion.

What I am arguing here is that, contrary to much of what has been written on the subject, favoritism can be a positive classroom force, but only if we teachers learn from what makes favoritism functional and apply some of its lessons in dealing with the rest of class. In short, we should find a way to allow us to think of some students as special (although perhaps more in personal interactions), but all students as equals: more *primus inter partes* than head-and-shoulders above the class. The teacher's pet is a good thing, placed in a personal context, and only becomes dysfunctional in the modern large classroom, where it translates into inequity that causes disruption for the rest of the class. I cannot therefore call—as some researchers have done—for the elimination or dilution of the teacher's pet because I see it as integral to the entire educational apparatus—not just teacher job satisfaction. Indeed, it is one gem passed down to us from the original model of the Platonic student-teacher continuing dialog. The lesson of all of this is that, if we as teachers may have in any particular course one student who is our special favorite, that does not mean that we are released from making the necessary extra effort to find enhancement items in the papers—and minds, hopes, and dreams—of all of our students.

NOTES

1. I have often joked with my colleagues that office hours are more fun than teaching; one-on-one interactions with students that allow extensive discussion (in the tradition of the Platonic dialog) are stimulating, presumably to the student as well. Obviously, the highly motivated, capable, high-achieving student is also more likely to show up to office hours and to be invited to "come by and talk about" topics of interest, including their career goals. Thus our oral extra-class commentary for such students may play as important a role in enhancing student-teacher relationships as what we write on their papers—in fact more.

2. I have heard many colleagues say, for example, that they like students from mainland China because they are "so hardworking and cooperative." It, therefore, seems to me that favoritism of that nature can work against the demographic realities

of modern teaching and thus become even more disruptive to the fair education that would normally be expected.

3. As noted most prominently by Lewis and Hastings (1992) as well as Pichaske (1995), at the other extreme of the teacher's pet phenomenon are relations based on mutual or one-way (harassment) sexual attraction or kinship ties (nepotism), or actual articulated hatred of race, ethnicity, or other demographic factors. All such relations cannot fall under our category because they compromise teacher volition.

WORKS CITED

Babad, E. "The 'Teacher's Pet' Phenomenon, Students' Perceptions of Teachers' Differential Behavior, and Students' Morale." *Journal of Education Psychology* 87 (1995): 361–74.

Baker, J. "Teacher-Student Interaction in Urban At-Risk Classrooms: Differential Behavior, Relationship Quality, and Student Satisfaction with School." *The Elementary School Journal* 100 (1999): 57.

Brophy, J.E. "Conceptualizing Student Motivation." *Educational Psychologist* 18 (1983): 200–15.

Engelberg, R.A. "Student Perspective on Grades." Ph.D. diss., University of Washington, 1988.

Frymier, A.B. and M.L. Houser. "The Teacher-Student Relationship as an Interpersonal Relationship." *Communication Education* 49 (2000): 207–19.

Fusani, D.S. "Extra-Class Communication: Frequency, Immediacy, Self-Disclosure, and Satisfaction in Student-Faculty Interaction Outside Classroom." *Journal of Applied Communication Research* 22 (1994): 232.

Guyton, D.C. "Good Teaching: Passionate Performances." *English Journal* 84 (1995): 59–60.

Keefe, C. "The Ethical Decision—Points for the Teacher in Relation to Student Perceptions of Unethical Behaviors." Paper presented at the 68th Annual Meeting of the Speech Communication Association, Louisville, Kentucky, November 4–7, 1982.

Lewis, John F., and Susan C. Hastings. *Sexual Harassment in Education*. 2nd ed. Cleveland, OH: Squires, Sanders & Dempsey, 1994.

Morgan, B.L. et al. "Students' and Professors' View on the Ethics of Faculty Behavior." Paper presented at the 104th Annual Meeting of the American Psychological Association, Toronto, Canada, August 9–13, 1996.

Moulton, P., M. Moulton, M. Housewright, and K. Bailey. "Gifted and Talented: Exploring the Positive and Negative Aspects of Labeling." *Roeper Review* 21 (1998): 153–154.

Orange, Carolyn. *25 Biggest Mistakes Teachers Make and How to Avoid Them*. Thousand Oaks, CA: Corwin, 2000.

Parr, M., and L. Valerius. "Professors' Perceptions of Student Behaviors." *College Student Journal* 33 (1999): 414.

Perlmutter, D.D. "Students Are Blithely Ignorant; Professors Are Bitter." *The Chronicle of Higher Education* 47, July 27, 2001; B20.

Perrine, R.M. "Please See Me: Students' Reactions to Professor's Request as a Function of Attachment and Perceived Support." *The Journal of Experimental Education* 68 (1999): 60–72.

Pichaske, D.R. "When Students Make Sexual Advances." *The Chronicle of Higher Education*, 41 (1995): B1–2.

Rickey, H.W., and M.H. Rickey. "Nonverbal Behavior in the Classroom." *Psychology in the Classroom* 15 (1978): 571–76.

Tal, Z., and E. Babad. "The 'Teacher's Pet' Phenomenon: Rate of Occurrence, Correlates, and Psychological Costs." *Journal of Educational Psychology* 82 (1990): 637–45.

———. "The 'Teacher's Pet' Phenomenon as Viewed by Israeli Teachers and Students." *The Elementary School Journal* 90 (1989): 96–108.

Van Horn, J.E., W.B. Schaufeli, and D. Enzmann. "Teacher Burnout and Lack of Reciprocity." *Journal of Applied Social Psychology* 29 (1999): 91–108.

Weinstein, C.S. "Teacher Education Students' Preconceptions of Teaching." *Journal of Teacher Education* 40 (1989): 53–60.

CHAPTER 5

Teaching Generation X: A Dialogical Approach to Teacher Commentary

Robert Samuels

Teachers' commentaries have been changing, and they will no doubt continue to do so in the foreseeable future. In this chapter, I will argue that institutional and cultural contexts are the most important determinants of the nature of comments teachers make, for they are the factors that help to shape the student-teacher relationship, especially in the writing classrooms. I will look closely at the social and subjective aspects of the current state of writing instruction and argue for the dialogical model of commentary that takes into account the particular demands facing insecure and untenured composition faculty. One of my primary areas of emphasis will be on the ways that the stress on student evaluations in writing programs alters the basic relationship between students and teachers. While the unstable nature of most writing positions creates a situation where the writing instructor must constantly monitor his or her interactions with students, the consumerist attitude of many "Generation X" students produces an environment of entitlement and defensiveness on the part of the "consumers" of higher education.

In his book *Generation X Goes to College*, Peter Sacks discusses this situation, whereby contemporary college students in America tend to press a sense of entitlement that leads to a low tolerance for any type of criticism or negative feedback. Sacks remarks that what these students, who have been raised by the entertainment industry, want is for their teachers to be friendly entertainers who do not challenge anyone's viewpoint or rude behavior (14). The moral relativism of postmodern culture motivates students to interpret many forms of teacher commentary as personal attacks on the student's particular style, and in the writing classroom, this sense of relativism is often heightened by the conflicting theories of composition and grammar that students encounter in high school and at college.

Anyone who has taught writing is familiar with the situation in which a student responds to a corrected paper by saying, "If that's how you want it, I'll do it. But every teacher tells me something different." While it is true that there are different theories of composition and that grammatical rules do change and vary, it is also true that students often cling to a relativistic belief system undermining most bases of conformity and authority. Grade inflation is one unfortunate consequence, when writing teachers, who rightly fear that students who receive bad grades will give bad evaluations, inflate grades and steer away from any type of critical commentary. Once established, the culture of grade inflation habituates students to demand only positive feedback and high marks. It is notable that it is those students who did not get the marks they desire who often over-react by refusing to read the comments that go along with the grade.

Adding to the difficult situation is the fact that many writing courses are required and thus they are not based on the students' personal interests or individual decisions. In a culture that celebrates individualism and freedom of choice, this universal requirement often places the teacher in the difficult situation of winning over the discontented student. Of course an effective way of turning this potentially negative situation into a positive one is to stress the positive aspects of each student's compositions. Student evaluations and grade inflation place the writing instructor in a very vulnerable position when it comes to making comments on student papers.

The conjunction between student empowerment and teacher disempowerment was manifest in an incident that occurred when I returned a paper that one of my students once wrote on *The Simpsons* television show that contained a number of anti-Semitic comments. When I remarked that the paper did not represent an academic response to the assignment, the student rejected my suggestion that he rewrite the paper by getting rid of all unsupported opinions; instead, he confronted me with the allegation that I could not have been objective if I was Jewish. Though I thought I had taken care of the situation when I stated that my religious affiliation had nothing to do with the assessment, I was surprised when the student's father called me up at home with threats. Among other profanities, he charged that I had no right to give his son a bad grade just because I disagreed with his viewpoint. All effort on my part failed to convince this particular father that his son's assignment was not an opinion paper, and he assured me that he had not given up the fight on his son's behalf.

Having dealt with the situation and settled the disagreement by refraining from making any further critical comments on this particular student's other papers—indeed in hopes of avoiding another conflict I had resorted to grade inflation—I was surprised when the student did not get over his grudges. He was the only student in the class who gave me a negative evaluation by stating at the end of the semester that I was intolerant of other people's opinions. Most shocking of all was that, several months later, it was this student's strongly worded recommendation that I be stopped from teaching entirely which featured prominently in the discussion of my teaching in the department's yearly review. Thus, though this particular case might appear to be an extreme situation, it brings clearly into focus some of the issues in student-teacher interactions that precipitate serious insecurities and anxieties for untenured faculty in regard to teacher commentary.

Among the sets of assumptions that I carry to my reading of student papers is the need to correct both mechanical problems, involving grammar and punctuation, and logic, coherence, and development of thought. Consquently, issues such as the misuse of commas and semicolons are of grave concern to me. Many of the problems connected with dealing with these sorts of mistakes in essays of students who are not mentally prepared to solve them in their work were amplified recently over an essay written by one of my students, whom I would like to call here by the fictitious name of Buffy.

While I was going over Buffy's essay with her, I noticed that she kept looking away from the paper. I asked to know the cause of her distraction, and she said: "First of all, this class is not a priority for me, and secondly, every teacher wants something different, so I don't see why you just don't tell me how to do it, so I can do it." I thought her response was not only pretty brazen but in a strange way very honest, since for many students, the required writing class is not a priority, and the feeling that every teacher makes up his or her own rules is pervasive. Moreover, it is not uncommon that students expect their teachers to tell them exactly what and how to write. In such a situation, if a teacher's comments do not give the students direct instructions, the students become upset and feel that they are not getting their money's worth.

On the first draft of Buffy's paper, I marked all of the mechanical errors and indicated where the rules are explained in our style manual. Nonetheless, her second draft reproduced all of the same mistakes. When I met with her again, I asked her why she did not make any of the requested changes. She responded by saying that the book was really stupid because it didn't explain anything and it was really boring. The book she was referring to is Diana Hacker's *A Writer's*

Reference, which might not be the most engaging read but does clearly state the correct usage of commas and semicolons. I soon realized, however, that Buffy's problem was that she did not know the meaning of any of the grammatical terms that Hacker uses to explain the proper usage of commas and semicolons. For example, she had no idea what an independent clause was; without this knowledge, none of Hacker's explanations could make any sense to her.

In connecton with this, I made another shocking discovery. I started to ask my students individually about independent clauses, cordinating conjunctions, introductory clauses, and restrictive elements. Virtually none of my students understood these terms; thus, all of my comments on their papers that referred to grammatical terms or Hacker's book were useless. Moreover, their lack of understanding of Hacker's explanations rendered my students frustrated and angry with me.

In response to this problem, I tried to explain the basic grammatical terms in class, but the students resented this boring subject matter, and they failed to learn the meaning of these terms in the group setting. From that point on, I decided to never hand back a paper without meeting with the student and discussing with the student the meaning and value of my comments. This dialogical model of commentary helps me to discover exactly what each individual student knows about grammatical and stylistic conventions. It also helps to build a personal relationship with the students, and it forces them to think about my comments by engaging in a conversation concerning their particular patterns of error.

This method may seem like it would be very time consuming; however, I have developed a process that does not require any extra time outside of the classroom. On the day that I will be handing back papers, I give the students a reading and writing assignment that they must complete in class. I then call each student up to my desk and discuss with each one all of the comments that I have placed on the papers. I try to limit myself to five minutes with every student who does not have major writing problems, and I schedule appointments with the students who need more help. One of the key elements of this method is to make sure that my commentary locates particular patterns of error and highlights the strengths of the paper as well as the parts that need further development.

I strongly believe that teachers' commentaries should be both encouraging and constructive. One way that I do this is to make sure that I start off my final comments by highlighting the positive aspects of the paper. For example, I often write: "You do a good job at responding to the assignment, and you have many strong points. The parts on subject X are well developed." These positive comments help the student to hear the next comments that are often directed toward patterns of error and the areas of content needing more development.

For instance, I sometimes conclude my final comments in the following manner: "You still need to develop the sections in paragraphs 5 and 7. You also have to work on commas, semicolons, word repetitions, sentence structure, and transitions."

By highlighting patterns of error throughout the paper and listing them in my final commentary, I am able to quickly discuss these problems with the student when we meet together. However, as the following list of the general responses that students have had to my final commentaries testifies, some students have a hard time focusing on my comments if they did not like the grade they have received:

1. I don't think my grade should be lowered because I used the grammar checker on my computer
2. You never told us that we had to use commas
3. My high school teacher told me to always use one tense
4. If you understand what I am saying, why does it matter how I say it
5. I don't think we should be graded down for grammatical rules that you haven't taught us
6. I corrected everything you told me to do, but I still got the same grade

Many of these student responses center on a denial of personal responsibility; they often blame past teachers, the current class, and technology for their own errors. This displacement of responsibility is a central aspect of postmodern culture, and it can be addressed through the dialogue that a teacher holds over the student's reaction to the teacher's commentary.

One way that our modern culture undermines personal responsibility is through the reliance on technological devices to correct human error. With the invention of computer spell checkers and grammar checkers, writers have started to place the responsibility for correct usage onto the machines that they are using. This shifting of responsibility is strikingly evident when students blame their computers and printers for their late papers. Teachers need to anticipate this postmodern problem by telling their students that these types of technological excuses will not be accepted.

Moreover, this cultural shifting of responsibility has helped to reshape the expectations that students have regarding themselves and their teachers. In order to explore this issue, I had two of my writing classes develop and distribute a survey that examined the qualities that students looked for in a good teacher and a good student. Each student in my classes had to ask ten other students from different classes what are the most important qualities for effective students and teachers. After the students had collected this information, I put them into small groups to analyze their data, and then each group presented their findings to the entire class. According to this survey and susequent analysis, here is the list of attributes that students most favor in an effective teacher: (1) open mindedness; (2) entertaining; (3) friendly; (4) interesting; (5) knowledgeable.

When we discussed these responses in class, students affirmed that the best kind of teacher is open to every student's ideas and does not act as a judge or authority figure. Furthermore, they added that the best way for teachers to respond to students' writing is to respect their ideas and give them friendly advice. They also agreed that the worst kind of teacher's commentaries were those that seemed like a criticism of the student's belief system.

The findings of this survey confirm Sacks's argument that Generation X students celebrate freedom of expression, individualism, and entertainment and that they dislike most forms of authority, criticism, and judgment. Surely these attitudes play an important role in the way that students receive teachers' commentaries. In fact, the changing ideas of what students expect from teachers are matched by the expectations that they have regarding themselves. In my students' survey, they found that the following qualities represent effective students: (1) comes to class; (2) open-minded; (3) good listener; (4) honest; (5) organized.

Perhaps the most interesting aspect of this list is that these attributes are primarily passive ones. Students feel that if they show up to class and listen to the teacher and their fellow students, they are being effective students. They also believe that the open-mindedness of the teacher should be matched by the open-mindedness of the students. I asked my classes why there was such a stress on open-mindedness and not on the particular knowledge or authority of teachers and students. Many of them responded to this question by affirming the right of every individual to express his or her ideas in a safe and affirming environment. This response made me think that students now want teachers to be more like talk show hosts than like authorities with a certain specialized knowledge.

The findings of my survey support Richard Straub's claims that he makes in his important essay "Students' Reactions to Teacher Comments: An Exploratory Study." In this work, Straub studied what kinds of teachers' comments students prefer:

Most of all, they appreciated comments in the form of advice and explanations. They liked all praise—even if it was only presented barely in the single-word comment "good" or presented in tandem with criticism. The best praise, as other researchers have indicated, was that which also provided reasons for something being good. Students also seemed to like comments in the form of open questions, especially when they were expressed in specific terms and presented in a helpful way. They did not appreciate straight or harsh evaluative comments—especially those dealing with content and those presented in general terms. (112)

In these observations, Straub's findings bear out the main arguments of Sacks's study that Generation X students love praise and hate criticism—especially if that criticism is directed toward their own ideas. As Sacks argues, the postmodern culture that questions all forms of authority and celebrates free speech and unlimited individualism can be largely held accountable for our contemporary students' conditioning (Sacks, 154–69). Furthermore, these students' attitudes also affirms the pragmatic American tradition based on the idea that problems should be just fixed and not overly analyzed.

This stress on the pragmatic nature of students is often evident in their desire for explicit remedies concerning grammatical problems. Straub reports, for example, that students see "judgments about grammar and sentence structure as matters of right and wrong," but they see "comments asking for a reconsideration of word choice as reflecting the idiosyncratic preferences of the teacher" (101). Indeed many students have responded to my comments on their papers by stating that writing classes should only be concerned with correct grammatical usage and not with the individual student's style or ideas.

What we need to keep in mind is that these students' resistance to criticism and authority has deep cultural and ideological roots. These students have been brought up in a society where every authority figure is constantly questioned and often undermined. Not only have they been affected by the break-up of the nuclear family and the post-Watergate suspicion of political power, they are also under the influence of the media and entertainment programs that glamorize the humiliation of authority figures. For these reasons, I believe that all current teachers need to take account of the diverse ways that the social and cultural forces in our society have transformed the basic relationship between teachers and students.

Straub found in his research that students do like teachers' comments that give detailed attention to specific aspects of the students' compositions. This need for attention may be also related to our "culture of narcissism" and the transformation of child-rearing techniques from discipline-based to care-based. Indeed, it may well be that the dialogical approach to commentary could produce such effects because it makes the individual student feel that his or her paper has really been read and given the teacher's full attention.

I want to illustrate some aspects of this approach in light of some actual conversations I have had with students regarding the comments I placed on their papers. The first relates to the use of open questions as my preferred mode of commentary:

Teacher: What do you think your main argument was in this paper?

Student: I'm not really sure. It was hard for me to figure out what to write because I am not used to expressing my own ideas in an academic paper.

Teacher: Well, this paper tries to get you to balance academic research with your own ideas.

Student: But how can you grade us on what we think?

Teacher: I'm not grading you on whether I agree with your ideas but how you do support your ideas with evidence and arguments.

Student: So, to get a better grade next time, should I just say what I feel?

Teacher: You need to explain and analyze why you hold these opinions and then you can enter into conversation with the academic sources you are referring to.

Through dialogue I was able to respond directly to this student's confusions concerning the assignment and the ways I grade papers that include the student's own ideas. This type of dialogical approach is necessary because students often have misleading notions regarding the ways that teachers grade and the exact nature of individual assignments. A dialogical approach thus helps the teacher to see what the student knows and how the student is interpreting the assignment and the general goals of the writing process. In addition, this type of conversation allows the teacher the opportunity to shift the student's attention away from grade toward an emphasis on revision.

In another variation of the dialogical method, I engaged a student in a conversation over her problems with comma placement:

Teacher: Do you know why you need to put a comma here?

Student: Because that's where I breathe?

Teacher: Do you know that this is an introductory clause?

Student: What's that?

Teacher: Well, if you start off a sentence by introducing the time or place of an action, you have to put a comma after the introduction ends.

Student: Oh! I didn't know there are rules for that, I thought you just put them when it sounds right.

Evident from this conversation is that we have moved from a text culture to a secondary oral culture. Students are increasingly basing language on what they hear in conversations and in the media and not on a set of rules and regulations; a dialogical approach to teacher commentary thus takes into account this cultural emphasis on oral communication at the same time that it stresses the need to respect the conventions of written English.

Dialogues with students over specific written comments enable the teacher to help break down the cultural difference between oral and written modes of communication. Through conversation the teacher also can improve his or her relationship with students by undermining the students' perception that the teacher is a harsh critic and authority figure who creates arbitrary rules and punishes students for not knowing these irrational conventions. It is a testimony to the power of conversation that it enables the teacher to enter into a reasoned discussion with his or her students, serving as one of the most effective ways by means of which Generation X students can be conferred a sense of recognition and connection.

Could it be the case that our current students feel such a great need for praise, recognition, and attention because they are often placed in large lecture halls, where no one seems to know who they are or if indeed they are even coming to class? Students who spend most of their days in large, impersonal settings habitually lose the ability to participate when they enter into smaller and more personal composition classes. Many of my students have said to me that they have become habituated to writing only what they think their teacher wants them to write, thus ignoring any of their own ideas and feelings. As is evident in the following dialogue, despite the best effort of the teacher, these students continue to feel conflicted over what position they should take in their own discourses:

Teacher: You start off this sentence writing "one"—singular noun—but you soon shift to the pronoun "they." Why do you do this?

Student: Well, I wasn't sure if I was supposed to talk about what I think or what everyone is supposed to think.

Teacher: Why do you think you were unsure about this?

Student: I never know if I am writing just for the teacher or for everyone or maybe just for my class, so if you say "one" or "they" you could be talking about anyone.

As can be clearly seen, the aim of this exercise was not for me to display my knowledge and to be able to wield its power over my student, inducing her submission, to make her stand in awe before the teacher. Rather, it was to engage the student in a conversation that helps clarify the student's own confusion. Significantly, in this dialogue, once again, the student not only shows a conflict over audience and voice but keeps on returning to oral characteristics of language. Through the dialogue, the student is able to grasp the possible cause of her own grammatical problem. She shifts references because she does not know who her audience is and she is unclear about what voice to take in a written academic paper.

I want to sum up by saying that the dialogical approach to teacher commentary recommends itself as one of the most effective ways of responding to student writing. It can sensitize the teacher into taking account of the cultural, institutional, and subjective forces that shape the current relation between teachers and students, and it can serve as one of the best means to bridge the gap between oral and written modes of communication. It is also one of the best methods by which the teacher can be successfully freed from the role of harsh critic and authority figure. Through the personal attention it gives to individual students, the dialogical approach can help transform written comments into live interactive forums that stress the collaborative nature of the revision process. As such, the dialogical method allows the teacher to give very specific advice and then see if and how that advice has been understood or internalized and used.

WORKS CITED

Hacker, Diana. 1989. *A Writer's Reference*. 3rd ed. New York: St. Martin's Press, 1997.

Sacks, Peter. *Generation X Goes to College: An Eye-Opening Account of Teaching in Postmodern America*. Chicago: Open Court Press, 1996.

Straub, Richard. "Students' Reactions to Teacher Comments: An Exploratory Study." *Research in the Teaching of English* 31.1 (1997): 91–119.

CHAPTER 6

A Shared Journey in Composition and Basic Writing Classes: Another View of the Dialogical Approach to Teacher Commentary on Student Assignments

Glenn Sheldon

In both my composition and my basic writing classes at The University of Toledo, I attempt to develop a dialogic approach to written comments on student assignments. I critique both formal essays and in-class writing assignments (mini-essays), and on both types of assignments, I include significant marginal, or side, or sidenote, comments. When I return the in-class writing assignments, I ask students to read the comments during class time, to consider them momentarily and to respond to them in class. I ask them to write me a short response to each of the content-based comments; this opportunity for their reactions sends a clear signal to students that marginal comments have value in the writing process. The goal is to to shift (however temporarily) students' emphasis from the grade to ways to improve their writing and thinking skills (which, in turn, results in a better opportunity to earn that desired grade).

As instructors, we know that if we "reinforce students' sense of themselves as powerless in their writing," they will not feel free to negotiate, for "the powerless cannot negotiate" (Horner 156). Negotiation with students, through the use of their reactions to teacher commentary, then, can empower them as writers. Although I find that some of my students believe the grade to be "the-be-all and end-all" of the writing process, the majority of them "rightly feel that they are entitled to more than just a few approving ticks in the margin" ("Marking Strategies").

The University of Toledo classroom may not be a universal site, but I suspect it can offer pedagogical parallels to other classrooms. It is an urban institution with a mix of the traditional, residential student and varied nontraditional populations. Race, class, and gender become important factors in the composition of its courses. Gaining trust from these students, then, is no simple matter. Balancing students' emotional needs with an obligation to give honest advice becomes a profound challenge that impacts classroom texts and the strategies of access. Using exercises that "talk back" to marginal, or sidenote, comments has often helped students to subvert monologic closure in favor of Mikhail Bakhtin's sense of dialogic expression; potentially, this can become a student's "entrance" into "interlingual contacts and relationships" (Bakhtin 11). In demonstrating that a text, any text, is not a closed system but an interactive one, students are introduced to the notion that honesty requires complex self-definitions of positionalities—theirs and their professors'. Students' creative flowering can be directly linked to their knowing that any text is an open, interactive one.

I introduce marginal notes as texts with an integrity of their own, as pieces with a special character and not merely supplemental directives. By opening the students' texts and allowing them a space for response, the simple idea that there is Truth (with the capital "T") is immediately challenged. By asking students about their writing strategies and not neccessarily their thesis, they are taught that the journey toward insight is more valuable than a concluding thought, and I work consciously in the classroom against "denying students any agency or power" (Horner 143). I encourage students to individually differentiate between themselves and the texts they create in the classroom and to know that criticism is about skill building and the means by which they can chart for their intellectual and emotional responses to primary texts.

I also utilize letter writing in my responses to formal essays, responses which I attach to the back of the essays and use as supplementary comments to the marginal notes, as an extension of the comments the students find sprinkled throughout their essays. Following is an example of a letter that I might attach to a formal essay. Generally, I make them shorter and more pointed than this, but I blend two sample letters together here to provide a wider range of types of critique:

Dear "Janet":
    This seems promising because your writing is generally clear and direct. However, organizational matters need further attention. You do need to rework your introduction; it should try to grab the reader's attention by putting forward its controlling ideas

up front. Your essay should go directly into your topic, instead of focusing on your process of thinking about beginning it. Otherwise, it is so easy to write empty words which do not add up. Begin with a specific idea of what you plan to discuss (your topic) and spell it out clearly—that is, get down to business.

Next, begin to build your case systematically. Avoid abstract and vague statements; add important details here (place specified). Write as vividly as you can. Remember, the reader wants to get a complete picture.

Rephrase your first sentence along these or other better lines (suggested changes included); it is awkward as it stands. I really hope you are using the Learning Assistance Center; before turning in your essays, get help there. Also, do you have access to a good grammar guide? You need to pay greater attention to technical matters such as grammar and punctuation (comma usage, sentence variation, etc.). Remember, it takes lots of practice to achieve perfection.

Thank you for sharing this personal experience with me; I applaud your courage in the face of adversity. Overall, you have made a very strong effort here that shows care and attention. The conclusion needs to be reworked, however. I think it is always best to avoid beginning concluding paragraphs with "In conclusion"; they are a sort of shorthand way of building a more complex paragraph transition (we discussed this last week; is that concept clear to you? If not, do come and see me and we can talk about that one-on-one). Can you think of a more complex paragraph transition that you can use? Like all skills, writing takes practice. So the more you practice, the better you become at it.

Glenn

As the letter makes clear, my comments highlight both the positive and the negative parts of the student's essay—what needs to be reinforced further or avoided entirely. I often ask students to respond to such letters, but not to the marginal comments, in short letters that state their reactions and insights. Although some letters express students' frustrations with how I have viewed the quality of their writing efforts, most express gratitude toward specifically targeting ideas that could use improvement. They do not confuse the criticism of their paper as a criticism of their experiences and/or intellectual responses.

Of course, I make it clear that students' responses are not graded, but that the responses are part of the overall course expectations. This tactic is not my invention, but expounds upon many of the insightful ideas included in Pamela Gay's article "Dialogizing Response in the Writing Classroom: Students Answer Back." I couldn't agree more with Gay when she states, "Teaching writing within a framework of answerability could include some articulation of what's going on behind our responses to student writing. We could put our words side-by-side and talk back and forth with our students rather than 'hold forth.'"

Students could use this "talk-back" form as a guide for talking with their teacher-reader and peers about their writing-rewriting process (Gay 10). In preparing for such "talk-back" in my classroom, I would have previously earned a degree of student trust that helps them believe me when I emphasize that I appreciate, in students' written responses as well as class discussion, an individual being forthright and opinionated. A classroom environment conducted in this manner, I find, leads students beyond assimilation of information and into accommodation, where learning can take place.

Trust, of course, is partly a matter of how well students "read" their instructors. In my experience, students quickly read and remember the overt and covert codes of each instructor; most of the students have clear ideas of the instructor's expectations and clearer ideas of what an instructor prioritizes. Students inscribe "intentionality" into classroom discourse, that is the teacher's intentions to help or punish them as readers and writers. Taking time out to encourage dialogue not only erodes some of the wrong impressions students can get into the habit of forming, it also breaks down power barriers so naturalized in the classroom and which impede learning (Kemp 193).

Any caring instructor must consider a variety of "pay-offs" before critiquing each and every assignment handed in. In the basic writing or development classroom, the necessity for subtlety increases; more so because, as Deborah Mutnick has noted, basic writing often "reveals cultural and linguistic differences in students who have been historically excluded from higher education" (146). Mutual trust and respect—earned by the instructor—contributes to the success of my methods. I do not try to earn respect, necessarily, but I come into the classroom respecting my students as individuals with challenging lives of their own, so I believe that contributes to the openness and trust most students extend toward me in return.

When I have taught Composition II: The African American Experience, for example, students are typically, and not surprisingly, taken aback that I am a white professor. After students get past the initial shock, they begin to see that I do not position myself as an authority on black culture but as someone eager to share what I know and to learn more. I have received the most amazing feedback from students who come to appreciate hearing a "white guy" talking so directly on issues of race. Indeed, I think it is my openness and directness in the classroom that students come to appreciate, and eventually, to trust.

In terms of my content sidenotes, I try to keep them brief and to the point. Realistically, students aren't going to read more than a phrase or a sentence's worth of criticism. I also tend to phrase my comments as questions, which helps to keep my criticism decentered from the professor/authority position. For example, I regularly teach Martin Luther King, Jr.'s, essay, "Letter from Birmingham Jail" in my basic writing courses, where I always provide a pointed essay question to guide the student writer. Inevitably, a few students hand in essays that generalize about their own accumulated knowledge of King (which is usually extensive in the classes that are predominantly African American). In such cases, I try to redirect the student writer back to the major points of the original, multipart essay question with comments such as the following: "I appreciate your overview of what you believe King to stand for, which very much agrees with my own view of his importance. Now, with this formulation, how can we begin to discuss how his character—as you and I see it—possibly leads him to persuade his dedicated followers to 'break unjust laws peaceably'? In short, from what you already know about him, why do you believe he chose this route?"

Although once I have had an angry reaction in which one particular student did not like my essay question and so was not going to answer it; in general, I usually receive more positive responses. Many students make the connection that essay questions offer more than mere guidelines—they force students to think more deeply about the subject and to reflect upon their writing. Such students take up the challenge gamely: They step up the type of analysis in writing that is taking place in class discussion. One of the more profound student responses stated, "In my high school, teachers would give you an essay question but they were always happy as long as you wrote about the general subject. I can see you want me to focus on more thinking about the essay, which, I guess, is what college is supposed to be about. Your question has forced me to do more thinking and more work, which is good because I want to be challenged in college." Typically, most responses fall between these two extremes; I often find that students make the connection that essay questions do more than serve as "guides"; they begin to realize that the structure of the question forces them to go into the type of analysis in writing that they find is taking place in class discussion. They want this because it meets their expectations of college as being more challenging and more open to diverse opinions.

It is important for students to know that all comments are open to discussion, that the remarks made on their work by the instructor are suggestions, not demands (particularly when these relate to differing interpretations of the text), but that each comment is made in the spirit of helpful advice; thus, all comments are worthy of consideration. Pamela Gay has said, "Dialoging response requires not just recognition of interpretive differences but a more complex recognition and 'admission' of multiple voices of our many selves and of the 'others' who are audience to our texts" (12). I am certain all institutions have their own institutional myths (akin to urban myths); one of The University of Toledo's (at least I believe it to be fictive) is of a writing instructor providing both good and bad advice on students' essays, and then instructing students to figure out which is which. If this is not myth, I would certainly welcome the instructor's rationale, for building mutual respect and trust cannot, I believe, include the notion that instructors may knowingly give erroneous advice. Advice to students may sometimes be considered "invalid" by a student

writer, but the intent behind advice to student writers must be well inten-
tioned, to say the least, and writing "must be taught as involving negotiation
about meaning" (Horner 162).

The main benefit from asking students to read and respond to teacher commentary immediately upon the return of their assignments is the assurance that
students read the comments. This practice also begins to allow the students to
think about whether some of my criticisms are valid or less than helpful and
why, thus helping to move them out of what Pamela Gay calls "the hostile re-
ceiver role" so that, again, in her words, they can become "active, willing participants" (9). Indeed, I encourage students to take only the suggestions that they
consider valid and useful in their revisions. In response to an essay on Albert
Camus's "The Sisyphus," for example, a student wrote: "If you can keep an
open mind, you can find happiness in the most absurd things." I responded that
this student writer's statement puzzled me a bit because it seemed to assume that
Sisyphus came to his punishment open-minded rather than that he came to
terms with it later. The student responded, stating that, in her opinion, Sisyphus always had an open mind in his creative trickery and thus came to his punishment similarly. In the revised version of this particular essay, I honored the
student writer's interpretation. After she received her very good grade, she
thanked me for actually not punishing her for "not agreeing" with her; subsequently, as the semester went on, she assumed much more of a leadership role
because she believed I honestly honored different opinions and interpretations.

Taking only those suggestions that students find valid appears to be easy for
them to do with peer critique; it is much more of a challenge for them to discard the instructor's advice. However, the character of the classroom, where
there are open exchanges of different opinions—not only among students but
among students and instructor—often gives student writers the confidence to
question instructor's advice. Also, in this scenario, it is important that instructors not automatically and systematically reduce grades based upon failure to
take instructor's advice during the revision process.

I habitually utilize two types of marginal notes on both formal and informal
essays. One type of note addresses some major surface problems, like grammar
or writing flow; another type of note addresses content critique, which is what I
ask students to respond to. With the in-class writing assignments, I address
only content so that the pressure of correct spelling and grammar is minimized.
However, more often than not, several students ask me to critique their in-class
writing assignments on both levels: content and surface. When students ask
me to simply make sure they aren't using run-ons or comma splices, I oblige.
For the in-class responses to my margical notes, however, the students are asked
to direct their attention to my content critique. That way, the student is ex-

pected to begin to understand that writing surface problems—while important—belong to a different type of revision process.

Ideas, insights, and analysis carry the weight of a college-level essay, and addressing them as such, with responses to sidenote comments, reinforces the notion that writing competency and critical writing success function on multiple levels. This helps students understand what Susan Miller calls "the variability of writing process" (118–119), by which, I think, is meant that in writing there is always room for improvement. Remedies to writing glitches, then, must be worked out on their own terms, at the level in which they function. Texts are always a series of negotiations.

Asking students to read marginal comments during class time, to consider them momentarily, and respond to them in class, sends a clear signal to students that the comments have value. Helping students to claim their significance(s) becomes a catalyst toward helping them to understand that "language mediates social reality and constructs our knowledge of the world and ourselves. The aim of writing instruction is thus to develop consciousness and control of rhetoric forms" (Mutnick 9). My marginal notes are not merely monologues or a list of demands (supplemental directives); they open student writers' texts and allow them room for maneuvers. The journey toward helping students understand that thinking and writing are unfinished negotiations leads them to feeling they have more agency in the classroom. Particularly profound in the basic writing classroom, students find more self-assurance and spaces in which to inhabit with their own voices. In both composition and basic writing classes, criticism becomes another step of skill building, and student writers often discover the means by which they can further their intellectual and emotional capacities to this new level of expectation.

WORKS CITED

Bakhtin, Mikhail M. "Epic and Novel: Toward a Methodology for the Study of the Novel." In *The Dialogic Imagination: Four Essays*, translated by Caryl Emerson and Michael Holquist, 3–40. Austin: University of Texas Press, 1981.

Gay, Pamela. "Dialogizing Response in the Writing Classroom: Students Answer Back." *Journal of Basic Writing* (Spring 1998): 1–17.

Horner, Bruce. "Rethinking the 'Sociality' of Error: Teaching Editing as Negotiation." In *Representing the "Other": Basic Writers and the Teaching of Basic Writing*, edited by Bruce Horner and Min-Zhan Lu, 139–65. Urbana, IL: NCTE, 1999.

Kemp, Fred. "Writing Dialogically: Bold Lessons from Electronic Text." In *Reconceiving Writing, Rethinking Writing Instruction*, edited by Joseph Petraglia, 179–94. Mahwah, NJ: Lawrence Erlbaum Associates, 1995.

"Marking Strategies." Mantex Information Design. http://mantex.co.uk/books/
     marks01.htm
Miller, Susan. *Textual Carnivals: The Politics of Composition.* Carbondale: Southern
     Illinois University Press, 1991.
Mutnick, Deborah. *Writing in an Alien World: Basic Writing and the Struggle for
     Equality in Higher Education.* Portsmouth, NH: Boynton/Cook Publishers,
     1996.

CHAPTER 7

Writing and Relationship

Marilyn D. Button

After teaching writing at the college level for over 18 years, I have become aware of many pedagogical innovations that I routinely attempt to deploy in tutoring student writing. But, with surprising and increasing frequency, students have continued to produce the same compositional errors. As a matter of fact, it appears as if, these days, my classes are filled with students more void than ever before not only of the ability to delight in the well-wrought phrase, but also of the skills of close reading as well as the capacity to generate stimulating essay topics. For someone like myself, who grades an average of 450 essays per semester, the question of how to respond to student writing assumes an acute importance. Why haven't the (by now) profusely abundant scholarly publications of the likes of Sommers, Knoblauch, Brannon, and Hillocks and others been more effective in helping teachers like myself in solving the problem of unpolished student writing?

Working on the supposition that investment schemes aimed at improving students' writing must be anchored first among the clients, the students themselves, I queried students representing a range of writing abilities—from developmental to advanced—in the form of a questionaire that required them to reflect on their experiences as budding writers.[1] Their responses were remarkably consistent in suggesting three basic principles as essential to successful writing instruction; they are the bases of my reflections as well as the tips that I propose in this chapter as the foundation upon which meaningful teacher commentary should rest.

First is that if teaching faculty do not establish a personal relationship with the students it proves difficult to motivate students to improve. Teaching faculty and students can develop a relationship through one-on-one conferences, classroom dialog maintained in person or through technology, and personalized feedback on student writing. In spite of limitations imposed by time, the relationship can even extend to a home cooked meal or an evening of basketball.

A second related principle is that even in the face of bad writing, positive feedback is crucial. Students can stand the bald truth about their writing, but prefer when it is delivered with kindness and by people whom they know to have their best interests at heart. A student's need for positive feedback suggests the ancient balance of presenting truth in love. Most people would appreciate such an approach in other circumstances; there is no good reason why teaching faculty would find its application to writing instruction undesirable.

Finally, the tougher the criticism, the better. Students consistently identified their best learning experiences as those that challenged them beyond their current abilities. Vigorously penned corrections, or strongly worded e-mails, were effective in signalling to students their need for grammatical correctness, stylistic improvement, and revision of thought. Generally, few students resist the challenge of high standards, and many resent the waste of time and money that easy courses represent. Predictably, many faculty who have a reputation for ruthless editing often have a coterie of devoted student fans.

Margaret Wheatley, alluding to quantum physics, has observed that the quantum view of reality has literally demolished the concept of the isolated individual and instead describes a world where "relationship is the key determiner of everything" (11). The nature of the relationships varies according to their respective "fields" or settings. In contrast to Newtonian physics, where life is perceived in dicrete elements, quantum physics presents a world where "subatomic particles come into form and are observed only as they are in relationship to something else" (11). Arguing that particles "do not exist independent of 'things,'" Wheatley asks: "If the physics of our time is revealing the primacy of relationships, is it any wonder that we are beginning to rethink our major issues in more relational terms?" (14). The value of positive, challenging relationships in education has been given a parallel endorsement by sociologists, psychologists, and theologians.[2]

Not even theorists, such as R.P. Feynman, who are skeptical about applying quantum physics to the discipline of writing, have failed to recognize the vital role that mentor-mentee relationships can play in students' intellectual growth.

Thus, Feynman warns about the danger that arises when "philosophical ideas associated with science are dragged into another field [where] they are usually distorted" (2) but concedes: "The best teaching can be done only when there is a direct individual relationship between a student and a good teacher—a situation in which the student discusses the ideas, thinks about the things, and talks about the things" the teacher wants him or her to learn (8).

The practice of using relationships to promote learning draws further authority from the fact that it goes back to antiquity. As someone who exerted influence on his scholar/learners through dialog and through his mentoring technique of eliciting, rather than inflicting, truth upon his pupils, Socrates could be considered the originator of the style of education rooted in relationships. Not surprisingly, the academic communities that were modeled after Socrates's ideas—the Academy, the Lyceum, the school Alexandria—became legendary for their phenomenal impact. While late Victorian England also popularized the idea that great literary achievement is often developed in a community (as shown clearly by the works of the Bloomsbury Group and the Inklings that were renowned as great masterpieces of literature), in our own time, editors, lovers, and co-authors all serve as co-creators and monitors of excellence. At the heart of a collaborative work's effectiveness is the notion, encapsulated in the contemporary variation of an African proverb, "It takes a village to write a book."[3]

A variety of social conditions are known to induce creative learning. For example, while some students respond well to humorous remarks cast at them casually in a writing laboratory, others prefer the more intimate and private approach of the personalized conference and the dialog that can occur through thoughtful journal writing and response. A colleague once described the power of relationships that are developed while walking around a classroom individually commenting on issues of style, grammar, or structure as students draft an essay. The effects achieved approach those of the more technologically oriented teaching faculty who deploy the virtual classroom using email and chatrooms as valuable fields of interaction.[4]

If, however, the teacher favors the written comment as the most effective means to instigate improvement in student writing, what should characterize such messages? Comments characterized by originality run the lowest risk of being ignored. In her important study of the end comment, Summer Smith affirms this conclusion based on her identification of three basic patterns of responses that she establishes as distinct genres. Recognizing that faculty responses to student writing fall into predictable patterns, Smith advocates a deliberate attempt to "resist generic conventions," and urges, "As teachers, we must heighten our awareness of the constraints of generic conventions and the danger they pose to end comments' effectiveness" (267). In particular, Smith asks all teaching faculty to "combat the negative effects of stability" because she believes that when end comments become predictable, they lose their effectiveness (267). The ideal comment reflects the reader's appreciation for the unique character of the writer, his or her purposes in writing, and the desired outcome of the writing exercise coupled with the reader's response to it. In crafting written comments, faculty can make deliberate grammatical and syntactical choices that influence the dynamic between writer, text, and evaluator and, therefore, must be sensitive in themselves to the various factors, including the power of the grade, that can influence the tone and content of the response.

Marginalia, as distinguished from end comments, can be used to enhance rapport between reader and writer. Marginalia can establish what Josephine Tarvers calls "the reader's consistent engagement with the text"; whether offered in "carefully phrased comments," or in the cryptic but more thought-provoking checkmark, this kind of feedback on student writing can be an exceptionally effective dialogic tool (143). This is what Kenneth Bruffee has in mind when he refers to the power of conversation at the heart of instruction.[5] Composition and literature instructors have now come a long way from the 1950s, when marginalia were used patronizingly as tools for affirming the possibility that the teacher found what students had to say important and even interesting.[6] Students would do well to consider themselves part of an erudite tradition that over the ages has helped in the intellectual development of great thinkers.

Many students already have a clear sense of their strengths and weaknesses and simply need an atmosphere in which such instincts can be explored without fear of failure. When, for example, some students respond gleefully to a returned paper with the remark "I knew you'd say that!" they are demonstrating their familiarity with the teacher's mind as well as an intuitive sense of what "works" and what doesn't "work" in their writing. The teacher's feedback serves merely to confirm their instincts. In such cases, the mentor/teacher might offer some encouraging remarks adapted from the preacher's wisdom in Ecclesiastes chapter 9, verse 7: "Go, eat your bread with a merry heart," and write your Expository Writing paper with pleasure, for God has already approved what you do.

When asked, students are willing to express ideas about their comment preferences. These ideas are critical to discussions of teacher commentary effectiveness because teacher commentary needs to strike a balance between students' feelings and productiveness. Many students, for example, need to hear, rather than to read, about the direction in which their writing should go. They are what some learning specialists call "auditory learners." To obtain good results, teachers are obliged to take account of the will of such students.[7] So must teachers be attentive to the notion that women are more inclined than men to clarify their thinking through dialogue—that they learn best by talking through their problems, rather than listening to or reading about other people's solutions.

All forms of response, both written and verbal, provide valuable opportunities to challenge and direct student thought. Feedback presents the chance to point to important truths in a way that is both personal and relational. The mode of the guidance must be dictated by the character of the student. Good writing evolves along with the development of the individual student, whose mental and emotional maturity has its own timetable. If teachers of writing recognize the range of personalities and abilities in their care, they will know that the hours of time spent reading and responding to student essays have merit according to the level of respect given the individuality of the developing writer. If, as William Glasser says in *The Quality School*, the great school is one in which students feel that teachers care, end comments and marginalia will spark interest and generate more improvement when students feel connected to the teacher as a person, when the students and their teacher are in a relationship. Without a doubt, therefore, the hours spent advising students on their writing will be enhanced by even small segments of time invested in other aspects of each student's life.

NOTES

1. This chapter is based upon information gleaned from questionnaires distributed to classes of varying competence levels: Advanced Writing, entry level Expository Writing, and remedial Basic English. For their help with other aspects of the research, my thanks go to colleagues at Taylor University, especially Dennis Hensley and Sonja Strahm, as well to Marie Nigro of Lincoln University of Pennsylvania.

2. For details on how nurturing friendships between students and teachers invariably lead to both parties working harder and producing better work, see chapter 9 of William Glasser's *The Quality School*. Educator and sociologist Ruby Payne, author of *Bridges Out of Poverty*, also confirms this view. And so does Einstein's theory of general relativity, which stresses that a community of learners enhances a fuller understanding of a given concept because it promotes a wider range of perspectives on any given subject than would otherwise be available.

3. For other concerns associated with collaboration among freelance writers, see Dennis Hensley and Holly Miller's *Write on Target*.

4. See Chris Anson's discussion of the vital role that technology can play in the virtual classroom.

5. See especially Bruffee's discussion of the role that conversation can play in cognitive development.

6. For a detailed discussion of the history of this attitude, see Robert Connors and Andrea Lunsford's very helpful survey of trends in composition research.

7. George Newell's research, though not gender specific, confirms the value of dialog in sharpening students' written responses to what they read.

WORKS CITED

Anson, Chris M. "Distant Voices: Teaching and Writing in a Culture of Technology." *College English* 61.3 (1999): 261–80.

Bruffee, Kenneth A. "Peer Tutoring and 'The Conversation of Mankind.'" In *The Harcourt Brace Guide to Peer Tutoring*, edited by Toni-Lee Capossela. New York: Harcourt Brace, 1998.

Connors, Robert J., and Andrea Lunsford. "Teachers' Rhetorical Comments on Student Papers." *College Composition and Communication* 44.2 (May 1993): 200–23.

Feynman, Richard P., Robert B. Leighton, and Matthew Sands. *The Feyman Lectures on Physics, Volumes I–III*. Reading, MA: Addison-Wesley, 1963.

Glasser, William. *The Quality School: Managing Students Without Coercion*. New York: Harper Perennial, 1998.

Hensley, Dennis E, and Holly G. Miller. *Write on Target*. Boston: The Writer, Inc., 1995.

Hillocks, George. *Research on Written Composition: New Directions for Teaching*. Urbana, IL: NCTE, 1986.

Knoblauch, C.H., and Lil Brannon. "Teacher Commentary on Student Writing: The State of the Art." *Freshman English News* 10 (Fall 1981): 1–4.

Newell, George E. "The Effects of Written Between-Draft Responses on Students' Writing and Reasoning about Literature." *Written Communication* 2.3 (July 1994): 311–48.

Payne, Ruby K., Philip DeVol, and Terie Dreussi Smith. *Bridges Out of Poverty*. Highlands, Texas: RFT Publishing, Inc., 1999.

Rothgery, David. "So What Do We Do Now?: Necessary Directionality as the Writing Teacher's Response to Racist, Sexist, Homophobic Papers." *College Composition and Communication* 44.2 (May 1993): 241–47.

Smith, Summer. "The Genre of the End Comment: Conventions in Teacher Responses to Student Writing." *College Composition and Communication* 48.2 (1997): 249–68.

Sommers, Nancy. "Responding to Student Writing." *College Composition and Communication* (May 1982): 148–56.

Tarvers, Josephine Koster. *Teaching in Progress: Theories, Practices, and Scenarios*. New York: Longman, 1998.

Wheatley, Margaret J. *Leadership and the New Science: Discovering Order in a Chaotic World*. San Francisco: Berret-Koehler, 1999.

CHAPTER 8

On the Margin of Discovery

Mary Theresa Hall

There is something enigmatic about approaching 25 years of teaching and still finding the job as exciting as when one began. In reflecting on the diverse ways by which my students' lives intersect and energize mine, mainly through the notes and remarks—both formal and informal—we exchange with each other, the topic of teacher commentary as a means of strengthening educational reform, therefore, is one I've been seriously thinking about lately for various reasons. The subject comes as a natural one for me to address at this point in my professional life because I can now begin to take stock of how the high school English and French classrooms (wherein I began my teaching career) and the English college classrooms (wherein I presently teach) shape and empower the discourse and pedagogy I share with my students.

Like many novice teachers, I firmly believed, when I began my career about 25 years ago, that my remarks—be they situated on the margins of students' papers, delivered orally in a corridor or classroom, or spoken offhandedly at a school function—were inherently worthy of respect and attention. I was more than eager to "right the wrong" answers on a French test and tweak the grammar and composition format in English essays to render them "correct and accurate" and to assure myself that I was, indeed, progressing along the path of becoming a master teacher. For the most part, my youthful enthusiasm and genuine desire to work with and teach adolescents were productive.

As "way led on to way," however, my initial fervor became displaced by such thoughts as: "Why don't these students already know this material? I have taught it three times today!" and "I wrote the same correction on this student's last two papers! Why doesn't s/he pay attention to my comments?" Eventually, what I considered "righteous indignation" in the late hours when I was reading student papers tempered my youthful enthusiasm and challenged me to engage other pedagogical strategies being touted at the time. Peter Elbow's theory of the teacher as simultaneously the prosecuting and defending attorney particularly extended a safety net that enabled me to balance the seeming contradictions and divergences that I encountered daily in the classroom. I became attentive to the power of verbal and body language in facilitating student achievement. I learned to be attentive, not only to the words on the students' papers but also—and perhaps more importantly—to the students' messages that permeated the pages, messages of confidence/confusion; triumph/anger; innocence/experience.

By writing seemingly innocuous marginalia and drawing distinct smiley faces that earned positive comments on student evaluations, I gradually acquired my own means of communicating with my students in a way that engendered their progress and distinguished my own teaching style.

One of the discoveries I have made is that while adolescence and young adulthood, like all major transitional passages in life, may be tempestuous and traumatic, the reality is that young people are natural seekers of truth and magnets of knowledge. Their curiosity and resiliency impel them to ask questions, wrestle with smugness, and rebel against complacency. Seemingly "macho" and "cool," these young men and women are inwardly vulnerable and sensitive, especially to language in all its nuances and manifestations. I wrestle with the questions of how best I could assess and evaluate each set of student papers and student presentations, and I begin with the truth acquired throughout my experience that all students, no matter their age and external facade, are terribly frightened of the critic, terribly sensitive to words of faint praise and harsh criticism, terribly alone in the vast desert of the blank page or computer screen, terribly intimidated by the sea of red ink that surrounds an alphabetical letter from A–F or an Arabic number of a grading scale; and just as terribly scared of receiving back a paper with no mark on it, save that of the letter grade or numerical value. As I operate out of these statements, how can I offer commentaries that both challenge and support my students whose emotional fragility seemingly overrides their resiliency and strength?

According to Peter Elbow, embracing opposites holds the key in providing a balance and restoring equilibrium. As Yeats says, "a terrible beauty" is born when humans wrestle with the creative and destructive forces of language. The indelible mark that is imprinted on the minds of the students in the transference of the printed, spoken, or unspoken word either forges manacles or opens passageways into the corridors of their creative and critical skills, the fostering of which, ultimately, is the role of the teacher.

Although handling a variety of preparations and student assignments in several different courses—including Introduction to the English Language (Linguistics), Introduction to Literature, Survey of British Literature I and II (all required courses for English majors and minors), English Composition, Honors English Composition, and a seminar on The Tragic Spirit in World Literature, places tremendous pressure on me to master my time so I may respond to note cards and assignments by the next day the class meets, I realize that the results far outweigh the discipline and inconvenience. For I have become convinced that all students deserve immediate feedback on their work, and more importantly, the teacher needs to demonstrate that work which is submitted in a timely, professional fashion, merits treatment in a timely, professional manner. For formal papers, essays, portfolios, and research papers, therefore, I respond to whatever hits my eye and evokes either agreement or disagreement because I believe that to read students' papers without offering praise or challenge is to do them a disservice. Where I encounter a statement or idea that requires clarification, I respond in a "sea of red ink," proclaiming their validity and ennobling the spirit of the student-writer. Since my goal is to stimulate the intellectual growth of all my students, I strive to maintain and convey, in all settings, a respect for them as people and for their work as it empowers and ennobles them. The remarks I write—both in the margins as I respond to a statement or paragraph and at the end of the paper in a commentary that accompanies the letter grade—are targeted toward improvement of their writing. I try to write as many helpful suggestions by commenting at length about the good points of each paper. I value thoroughness in commenting on papers, and I feel free to offer praise and compliments on how students have progressed throughout the semester. I prefer comments that are fair and balanced; therefore, I describe both the strengths and weaknesses, and I give helpful suggestions on how students can improve both their thinking and writing. I make myself readily available for consultation and help. At first, some students may not like the rule that they wait 24 hours after I returned their papers to discuss the paper with me, but as the semester goes on, they begin to appreciate having this time to read my comments and suggestions and the deadline for revising their paper or project.

I put a great deal of time, energy, and concentration on writing commentary and discerning the central voice out of which each writer speaks, so I need to stay focused on the papers I am currently assessing. To this end, I require that all papers for a particular assignment be submitted on the due date. (Students with unexpected illnesses and emergencies must report them to me via a note, e-mail, or phone call if they want to receive a letter grade; otherwise, all late papers are given extra credit points but no letter grade.) I emphasize the necessity of remaining focused when reading and working on assignments; my rule of holding students accountable underscores the emphasis I place in class on accountability, collegiality, and collaboration.

Quite literally, the responses I make on student papers allow me the opportunity to "talk" to my students, some with whom I would not ordinarily engage in such discourse. More consistently at the beginning of each semester and then sporadically throughout the semester, I issue a note card to the students each day the class meets. On it, I ask them to respond to a reading selection for the current class by addressing such questions as:

- Do you think John Donne or George Herbert deserves the title of "father of metaphysical poetry?" Can you suggest another seventeenth-century author also deserving of this title?

- Of the two poems and two short stories you read for today, suggest one from each genre that may be considered companion pieces and provide your rationale.

- Explain the process you undergo in writing a rough draft. Refer to the model (suggested on p.____ in your Composition text) and discuss how you do or do not find it helpful in developing your style of essay writing.

Such questions elicit honest, straightforward responses because the students address the question(s) I pose in a limited time frame, using their own critical judgment and serving as the "expert" on each question. These kinds of questions allow the students to co-author and critique the reading selections in a manner far different from those questions requiring solely rote memorization or those questions that focus exclusively on symbolism, theme, plot, or authorial biography. Their responses to these note cards enable me to get to know my students very quickly at the onset of each semester as I respond with a ✓+, ✓, or ✓– to each note card (the significance of each check mark is explained), and a written comment as to the depth of response and accuracy of information conveyed. I always direct my comments to the students by name, praise a remark that I find particularly good, encourage their critical reading, and tell them that I look forward to working with them throughout the semester. (Students who are absent respond to the questions via e-mail, and I reply as soon as I receive their e-mail.)

As the semester evolves, I continue to encourage this kind of thinking and to elicit student responses that are different from mine and from what their texts or the critics suggest. Students soon begin to pay serious attention to the specific literary selection under consideration for "proof" that authenticates their position; they revel in their new-found role of "critic," a role that they initially resist. As a result of beginning the semester with this type of informal correspondence, students become accustomed to and actually anticipate the responses I write on their rough drafts or other forms of assessment. Students who become habituated to reading my comments follow this pattern throughout the semester.

In my experience, students respond more positively to comments and marginalia that are specific—"Good introductory paragraph with well-formulated thesis statement"—rather than general—"Good opening." They respond angrily to sarcastic, terse remarks such as, "Do I need to explain semicolons and colons again?!" I am quite liberal with placing single or double checkmarks over words or in the margins of sentences or paragraphs that I think are particularly well written; that provide a clear, strong argument; and that underscore the paper's thesis.

If a sentence on a student's note card, essay, or assessment paper merits a response— "I think that some of the questions for our note cards were too general, and need to be more specific if the purpose is to test whether the students read and comprehended the material"—I write a marginal note—"Part of my rationale in providing the note card is to get to know students' names and writing styles at the onset of the semester, not so much to test content."

Sometimes a single word or a few words may be sufficient, for example, "Exactly!"; "Great!"; "Excellent, thorough analysis"; "Use textual citations to prove your point here"; "Refer to the handbook for punctuation, especially use of colons and semi-colons"; and "Yes, I'm glad you refer to and use this handout [I distributed in class]"; "Congratulations on a well-deserved grade!" But, especially at the beginning of a semester, students ultimately profit more from explicit, direct remarks that pinpoint as accurately as possible their specific strengths and weaknesses.

I particularly enjoy writing commentaries via e-mail. The following is an excerpt from an e-mail response I wrote to a student who was absent from an Introduction to Literature class and who submitted a poem via e-mail for extra credit:

Dear [name],

Thank you very much for the e-mail. I really like the poem (you received +10 E.C. points for it) and appreciate your sharing it with me. I thought you did an excellent job with your presentation on Thursday and was so proud of your confidence and the material you covered. Thank you for providing a very good lesson and model for subsequent presentations. Please give me your note card tomorrow, with a response to your presentation, the grade you think you deserve and why. And, finally, a reminder that your Literary Response Portfolio is due tomorrow. [This information also appears on the course syllabus, but this serves as a reinforcement.]

I hope you're feeling better. See you tomorrow. Thanks again for the e-mail.

Electronic mail, marginalia on student papers, one-to-one or group conferencing—today's educational system allows us to communicate with students in so many ways—provide a range of opportunities to offer educated suggestions by which our writers' purposes and meaning may be conveyed and which alert us to the ways by which our reading of and responses to student writing vary from student to student and from writing to writing.

During this past year, I created what I term an Assessment Analysis Tool, which enables me to receive the students' own personal and critical responses to a piece of writing. Before they submit an essay or paper, I ask them to critique in writing their responses to the following questions on the reverse side of their paper:

1. Of what are you proud in your essay?
2. How did this essay challenge you as a writer? As a literary critic?
3. What are the strengths of your essay?
4. What are the weaknesses of your essay?
5. How did peer and instructor collaboration and conferencing assist or hinder you?
6. Any statements or concerns you have about this essay? About anything in the course to date?
7. Questions or suggestions?

These questions enable the students to proofread their paper one more time before submitting it, to assess it from a more critical perspective, and to dispassionately express their pride or disappointment in their writing process/product. Many times, their responses to questions 5 and 6, in particular, alert me to specific issues that clarify the challenges and limitations of the mode of instruction, the progression of the course, the instructor, and/or the students. These responses also make me aware of "technical" problems the students encountered in the assignment, problems with MLA format, placement of the header, and other issues of which students are conscious but for which, without my knowledge, they would ordinarily be penalized if the product were inaccurate.

I also factor in these responses—and the manner in which they are written—in determining the grade of the paper. When the students receive their graded papers, I distribute portfolios (I have used portfolio assessment quite frequently in my teaching career) and ask them to record their responses to these questions on a sheet of loose-leaf paper which remains in their portfolio:

1. Are you pleased with the assessment of your paper: grade, comments, suggestions?
2. In your critical assessment, was your paper graded fairly, according to the classroom discussion, checklists, and grading criteria (provided at the end of the course syllabus)?
3. What will you do differently to strengthen the next paper?

These two types of student assessment—the former, written before the paper is submitted, and the latter, upon written receipt of their graded paper—empower student writers to serve as their own "defending and prosecuting attorney" in short, to become critics of their own thinking and writing. As one student responded: "The assessment folder [portfolio] helped me to recognize my own growth as a writer, keeping me informed of the positive changes I have made throughout the semester."

By critically assessing their own writing as well as my comments, the students acquire ownership over their work in a more comprehensive manner that incorporates shared responsibility, collaboration, personal decision making, mutual respect, and accountability in the writing and critical thinking process, thus enabling them and me to dispassionately critique their work as it evolves.

As part of the final exam grade in each course, the students write what I term a "self-assessment paper." The students are asked to review the contents of their portfolio and

in this self-reflective essay, discuss how your creative and analytical skills, writing ability, self-confidence in communication and in your major have been enhanced as a result of specific readings, assignments, presentations, and writing you have completed for this course. How has your writing style (as demonstrated in your Literary Response Portfolios, critical response papers, exams, the research paper . . .) changed and matured? How will effective writing and oral communication skills enhance your major? Your intended profession? Use our texts(s), research, class notes to authenticate your viewpoint. This paper is to be typed, double-spaced, approximately three-to-four pages in length.

To be perfectly honest, this is the paper I most enjoy reading at semester's end. These papers consist of such statements as:

Throughout the semester, I have found that a broad spectrum of writing techniques and a diverse selection of readings were incorporated into English Composition. The class was challenging and gave me the opportunity to develop my own writing style, as well as learn how to evaluate others. . . .

The note cards were a good incentive at the beginning of the semester to complete the reading. The questions effectively evaluated our reading skills and provided a simple way to improve our grades. . . .

Not only have I found this assessment essay to be interesting, but it also made me appreciate how much I have done, learned, and accomplished this semester. I think that it provided valuable insight into my progress as a writer and allowed me to review my strengths and weaknesses. At first, I did not see how Dr. Hall or I could benefit from this [assessment] paper, but after analyzing my essays, books, notes, presentations, research paper, and note cards, I realize that this paper expresses how thoroughly the objectives of the course have been completed.

Clearly, communication between my students and me occurs consistently throughout the semester. The written comments that occur between us are regarded with seriousness of purpose and intent and are conveyed in a manner that is respectful, supportive, and challenging. Since focused reading, responding to, and commenting on student writing is quite time-consuming, it is imperative that we convey, both orally and in writing, skillful and cogent insights that affect student creativity and invention. By giving students a voice and demonstrating that their words matter, teachers share their power to affect in a positive way the learning environment in the classroom. They validate divergent thinking; encourage—give heart to—student self-actualization; empower their students to communicate with more confidence, assurance, and honesty; and meet their students on a brave new margin of discovery.

WORKS CITED

Elbow, Peter. *Embracing Contraries: Explorations in Learning and Teaching.* New York: Oxford University Press, 1986.

Leach, Leslie R., Nancy A. Knowles, and Tracy D. Duckart. "Living the Myth: Merging Student and Teacher Needs in Responding Effectively and Efficiently to Student Papers." Paper presented at the Annual Conference of the English Council of California Community and Two-Year Colleges, San Francisco, California, October 16–18, 1997.

Straub, Richard. "Students' Reactions to Teacher Comments: An Exploratory Study." *Research in the Teaching of English* 31 (1997): 91–119.

CHAPTER 9

Teacher Commentary:
Put That Red Pen Down for Now!
Louise Maynor and Sandra Vavra

Composition and literature teachers are easy to identify and pity; their desks are covered with piles of student papers waiting to be graded. Like faithful packmules, they regularly haul these essays between office and home in brief-cases and tote bags. Despite their best efforts to write precision analyses, the endless hours devoted to fostering dialog with students often come to nothing. Many students choose to not pay attention to comments aimed at improving their writing. Of the many reasons offered to explain why teacher commentary pays little dividends, perhaps the most persuasive is the claim that "product-centered, judgmental responses have overwhelmingly remained the norm" (Podis and Podis 91; see also Knoblauch and Brannon; Elbow; and Straub and Lunsford).

Nancy Sommers confirms this by stating that the majority of teacher commentary is hostile and mean-spirited (149), and Mina Shaughnessy lends support to this line of reasoning when she says that teachers tend to look at student papers with "a lawyer's eyes, searching for flaws" (7). Because Peter Elbow claims that instructors who are "bitter or unforgiving or hurting toward their own work . . . are most critical and sour about student writing," he suggests that these instructors first find ways to like their own writing before they tackle student papers (409). While Margot Soven feels that teachers "overcorrect be-cause of their blind adherence to the 'rules of good writing'" (112), Lil Brannon and C. Knoblauch conclude that "instructors tend in their responses to appropriate students' texts, devaluing them in relation to some 'Ideal Text' the instructor had in mind" (158–59). In a random sampling of 3,000 papers, Robert Connors and Andrea Lunsford found that instructor comments were principally, and defensively motivated, "grade justifications" (201).

It is interesting to note that, in additional research on writing teacher com-mentary, the National Association for Educational Progress and others have confirmed that no significant difference in student writing improvement exists between teachers who mark papers extensively and those who make only a moderate number of corrections (Soven 111). Perhaps it is awareness of this re-ality that has compelled Jackie Proet and Kent Gill to conclude that "if [cor-recting] is done by the teacher with no further response from the student, it is probably a useless activity" (25).

If the research that finds that teacher commentary has been woefully mis-used as a tool in pedagogy is valid, teachers face a dilemma: Should they discard this feedback tool completely, or do they reflect upon how it may have been misused so that they can modify it? As the exploration begun by recent scholar-ship suggests, teacher response to student writing can be a highly useful source for student writing improvement if teachers commence formative, reflective response early in the writing process (Elbow; Straub and Lunsford).

What this kind of feedback requires is that teachers abandon their search for a unified set of practices, such as holistic scoring or primary trait scoring, which seem to promise objectivity but, in fact, do not deliver. Instead, teach-ers might consider a point of view that accepts context-dependent commen-tary that honors the varied personalities and skill levels of their students and, at the same time, complements the specific requirements of a diverse array of writing assignments.

To adopt the kind of flexibility promoted by the context-dependent ap-proach to teacher commentary is not to abandon time-tested theoretical guide-lines in favor of informally generated formulas. Flexibility does not necessarily mean that teachers will abandon their role as gatekeepers of academic stan-dards. Flexibility simply entails that teachers remain faithful representatives of their discpline but find ways to use more effective strategies in helping their students improve their writing—strategies that, in Peter Elbow's words, "dislodg[e] the emphasis on error hunting or pushing student writing into the synthetic mold of the five-paragraph theme" (381). As Professor Elbow adds in the same passage, one such strategy is to "champion a less criterion-based way of responding to students' writing that deliberately avoids the didactic efflu-ence of the red pen" (381).

We like to endorse the pedagogy of the teacher who functions as piano instructor (a metaphor first suggested by George Hillocks) and the writing teacher as parent. Such a dual role, we believe, obliges the writing teacher to pare down judgmental feedback to the barest minimum. As maintained by Hillock, the piano teacher's evaluative feedback is so "selective"; rather than pointing out every misplaced note, the piano teacher focuses on a few problems and only those which the student has demonstrated he or she can correct (195). Hillocks recommends an average of five to ten hours of independent practice to one hour of guided practice during each lesson, specifying that evaluation is only one part of an entire lesson, the bulk of which is devoted to listening carefully as the student describes problems he or she is having with a particular piece. Since the teacher plays the instrument along with the student, in addition to planning what piece the student will practice during the next week as well as discussing feelings about the work, Hillocks advises that piano students remain with particular teachers for as long as possible in order to nurture the significant communicative relationship engendered through a mix of compliments and criticism (196). Learning to write is not exactly the same thing as learning to play music; however, the composition teacher can use the kind of love that the piano teacher shows for both music and music students. When composition teachers listen carefully to their students, they can foster a relationship of mutual trust and respect that in turn increases student interest in the subject.

The writing-teacher-as-parent metaphor is equally rich in behavorial implications that go well beyond the fiduciary responsibility indicated by the term *in loco parentis*. James Moffett and Betty Wagner, after considering how young children learn at home before they attend formal schooling, conclude that children learn all day, all the time, at rates of knowledge acquisition far greater than they will ever achieve any other time in their lives (47). Since parents are the first teachers, reflecting upon how they perform this role seems a useful activity for writing teachers. The common example of children learning to walk is instructive.

An eleven-month-old child trying to take the first steps, for example, practices on its own schedule, not to a set time frame. During the times the parent observes the child attempting a step, failed attempts are praised rather than criticized; if a parent notices that a child's attempts work better in a particular location—for example, near a piece of furniture where the child can safely lift itself up and then hold on while getting balance—the parent may ofer "feedback" to the child by moving it to the spot that provides optimal conditions. Wise parents know that if their child doesn't walk exactly at the same time as its older siblings did, or when the neighbor's child did, this particular child is not a failure. They know that learning to walk is not a competition and that walking does not require pointing out errors in technique to learn. As such, parents simply continue to observe, praise, encourage practice, and offer feedback until the child masters the skill.

Moffett and Wagner say that language development, which proceeds at exponential levels from infancy to school age, is the result of a supportive, non-error-hunting learning environment:

The child initiates speech efforts and gets feedback, on the basis of which she modifies her speech. Such parent-child interactions have been recorded and studied and demonstrate beautifully the action-response-revision model of learning that a warm, spontaneous, responsive environment gives. People don't shame [the child] if she speaks ineptly, so she dares try over and over until she gets good. (47)

This faith in the child's perseverance and natural ability to master the skill is the antithesis of the mean-spirited error hunting that research has uncovered in many a teacher commentary. So, it seems reasonable to conclude that the first step toward providing students useful feedback is to assume the point of view of a parent and the stance of a piano teacher. With these approaches, the teacher is more apt to "like" something in each student's writing, in the sense that Peter Elbow uses the term.

Indeed, Elbow, speculating upon what motivates adult writers to continue working on a piece rather than abandoning it, explains what "to like" means:

We write something. We read it over and we say, 'This is terrible . . . but I *like* it. Damn it, I'm going to get it good enough so that others will like it too.' And this time we don't put it in a drawer, we actually work hard on it. And we try it out on other people too—not just to get feedback and advice but, perhaps more important, to find someone else who will like it. (405)

Elbow claims that published writers are those who are "driven by how much they care about their writing" (406). Once they learn first to like a piece, even though it may need massive revision, the next indispensable step is to find an appreciative reader whose feedback the writer needs to improve further. In conclusion, Elbow states emphatically: "Good writing teachers like student writing and like students" (406).

Liking student writing seems to be common sense, but it is not an easy thing to do because the conditions under which many teachers perform are often difficult and unnatural. When students, unlike professional writers, are not in a class by choice, it is difficult to motivate them—more so when the teacher has stacks of papers (some times up to 100 or more a week) to mark and return. It is also difficult for teachers to replace error hunting with something as clearly nonrigorous and nonacademic sounding as "liking" because such a practice would seem an invitation for teachers to renege their responsibility to teach students to make the kind of sharp discriminations between good and bad writing teachers customarily feel called upon to make. In short, would not negotiating between "liking" and the sort of critical judgments teachers want to foster about good writing present real problems?

Upon close examination, Elbow's defense seems persuasive after-all—especially in light of his argument that it is a more exacting kind of discrimination to see the potential in a piece of writing rather than its faults. We also agree with him that there is much composition teachers can learn from the methods B.F. Skinner deployed in teaching pigeons to play the game of ping-pong:

> How did he do it? Not by moaning, "Pigeon standards are falling. The pigeons they send us these days are no good. When I was a pigeon . . ." He did it by a careful, disciplined method that involved close analytic observation. He put pigeons on a ping-pong table with a ball, and every time a pigeon turned his head 30 degrees toward the ball, he gave a reward. (Elbow 198)

A look at what students write in personal letters may further enable us to understand why it will be more productive to spend time looking for what is positive than hunting endlessly for errors in student writing.

The personal letter—the tool that women used to make themselves literate when society dictated that only men should receive formal schooling—is especially suitable to be used as a test case because it is the most likely vehicle in which young people develop a writing voice and employ rhetorical strategies such as accessing audience and adapting style and diction to purpose. Because extravagancies are permissible in letters that would be unbearable in real-life conversations, one can take language to the limit in a letter. Yet, as indicated by the following letter that one student addressed to a friend she hadn't heard from lately (in which she meanders from one topic to another without imposing a proper sense of order on her rambling thoughts), the letter-writer would be wise not to push the elasticity of the form to an absurd level:

Dear Brittney,

I was worried because I haven't heard from you in three weeks. What's up? Guess what? I went to the Backstreet Boys' concert the other night. It was awesome. I know you prefer groups like Beck and Korn, who write lyrics which are relevant, but I think you would have liked the way Boys jammed anyway. How are things at school? I'm doing okay, though math is freakin me out. I hope you can write back soon. I really miss talking to you every day.

Bye for now, Tameika.

Instead of focusing upon the obvious weaknesses of this letter—the lack of focus, wrong word choice, and imprecise diction—response from the perspective of teacher-as-parent spotlights its potential value. Such a teacher begins with an enthusiastic comment about what's good about the content, voice, tone, and purpose of this letter, pulling no punches in its criticism. The teacher spends more time filling in the details, just as he or she would with friends in a face-to-face conversation. Students accept this kind of criticism as a meaningful, relevant, and useful guidance for revision because it is stimulating rather than grueling or defensive.

In a recent assignment, for example, one of us asked a group of advanced composition students to write an argumentative paper that considered an audience that might be hostile to the writer's point of view. One student wrote as follows in the prewriting outline of the assignment:

I am writing an argumentative essay to inform my readers on the out of control state of urban police forces. I was considering a tone that might be rational but after the Diallo verdict it is imperative that I be as persuasive and emotional as possible. I am angry and I feel an overwhelming sense of urgency to voice my concerns about the brutal and wanton display of power upon my fellow black brethren. I could be that innocent victim of police brutality before my essay is complete. I truly believe that a million black men could be killed in the same manner as Diallo and whites wouldn't flinch a bit. They would sit at their table and eat Hamburger Helper. Little Suzie will watch Rugrats. All the while a black mother mourns the senseless execution of her only son. I have done extensive historical and factual research for this paper, probably more than necessary. I guess there are those that will reason against my position with something like an argument for social benefit ("hopefully the Diallo verdict will send a message to the darkies—don't [mess] with the masters!!").

Rather than provide prescriptive comments on what the student failed to do correctly, we sat down with this particular student, and read the journal entry together. During the conference, we emphasized the material we liked in the entry: the passion for the topic and the overwhelming number of illustrative cases the student was able to build in the paper. We, of course, prodded this student gently to be mindful of the fact that the hyper-emotional, accusatory, and generalizing tone of the paper was likely going to turn off even a disinterested reader. There was no mention of grammar or punctuation. During several revisions, we continued to find ways to focus on the positive things in the paper: the particular cases highlighted, the reflections on the accumulative evidence, and the increasingly poignant tone, which emerged as the student writer worked hard to avoid lecturing, relying instead on the emotional impact of the examples. We deliberately limited discussions of usage and punctuation, and we asked the student writer to take the lead in asking directed questions: Is this the proper use of the bracket here? Am I correct in using "that" here, for a restrictive clause?

Everything fell into place. The final draft was a controlled piece of carefully orchestrated case study which made a compelling argument without preaching or pointing fingers at the audience—far from the accusatory voice in the journal entry. There remained a few surface errors, but there was no doubt that the student had considerably reduced the number of errors in the paper. Here is an excerpt from the student's comment in a debriefing journal entry written after the paper was completed:

Teacher comments have allowed me to examine my style while re-examining the messages I am trying to bring to the audience. This has allowed me to see an improvement not only in my writing, but also in my personal self as a whole. Prior to writing my argumentative paper, I was ready to spew out invectives to anyone who would listen. I felt relieved, but the role of my paper was so that I was able to change the tone without sacrificing the message or my passion.

Successful efforts like this one have convinced us that as writing teachers we should provide suggestions that inspire rather than discourage; for that reason, we try to provide feedback orally through discussion as much as possible and as early as possible in the writing process. Related to this issue is our discovery of the need to give students as many opportunities as possible to comment on their own writing.

By giving student writers the chance to analyze their own work, instructors not only allow student writers to maintain control of their own writing but provide a perfect protocol analysis of what student writers understand about the subject matter of their papers and the writing processes. It is a strategy that works particularly well in regard to literary analysis. Under this method, the instructor begins by immersing students in several works by one author and then spends some time discussing the predominant stylistic elements (e.g., tone, sentence structure, diction, imagery, and recurring themes) of the particular author's writing. Students are then assigned to write either a parody of one of the works or an original piece in the style of the featured author. Once the piece is written, each student is asked to identify the stylistic element he or she used in developing his or her piece and describe its purpose, or at least what the element was supposed to achieve.

The method by means of which student writers are asked to compose and then deconstruct their compositions is not only a far better way to sharpen their discriminating skills, but it is also a far better way to channel growth in creativity of student writers than teacher commentary that is focused on error hunting and prescription that approriates students' texts. However, teachers who decide to give teacher commentary primacy must give comments that student writers can use. Waiting to comment on what might be revised just as a grade is affixed to a paper is both unfair and counterproductive to learning. Placing the commentary and criticism at the beginning of the writing process, rather than at the end, gives students feedback they can use. Providing oral commentary, during formal conferences and through brief informal comments in class, sets up the meaningful reader-writer dialog that is vital to deep revision. The time usually spent on writing laborious comments on papers can be better spent giving early drafts close readings that identify what students can capitalize upon in the next draft. Offering pointed spoken comments to students early in the writing process is far more valuable than a postmortem affixed to the final grade. Summative assessments can then be made by a quick, holistic reading—no more than a few minutes for a typical paper—without the pressure of marginal or end comments to justify the grade.

WORKS CITED

Anson, Chris M. "Reflective Reading: Developing Thoughtful Ways to Respond to Students' Writing." In *Evaluating Writing*, edited by Charles R. Cooper and Lee Odel. Urbana, Ill.: NCTE, 1999.

Brannon, Lil, and C.H. Knoblauch. "On Students' Rights to Their Own Texts: A Model of Teacher Response." *College Composition and Communication* 33 (1982): 157–66.

Connors, Robert J., and Andrea Lunsford. "Teachers' Rhetorical Comments on Student Papers." *College Composition and Communication* 44 (1993): 200–23.

Elbow, Peter. "Ranking, Evaluating, and Liking: Sorting Out Three Forms of Judgment." *College English* (February 1993): 187–206.

Hillocks, George. *Research in Teaching Composition*. Urbana, Ill.: NCTE, 1986.

Knoblauch, C.H., and Lil Brannon. "Teacher Commentary on Student Writing: The State of the Art." In *The Writer on Her Work*, edited by Richard L. Graves. 2nd ed., Upper Montclair, NJ: Boynton/Cook, 1984. 285–91.

Moffett, James, and Betty Jane Wagner. *Student-Centered Language Arts and Reading, K–13: A Handbook for Teachers*. 3rd ed. Boston: Houghton Mifflin, 1983.

Podis, Leonard A., and Joanne M. Podis. "Improving Our Responses to Student Writing: A Process-Oriented Approach." *Rhetoric Review* 5 (1986): 90–98.

Proett, Jackie, and Kent Gill. *The Writing Process in Action: A Handbook for Teachers*. Urbana, Ill.: NCTE, 1986.

Shaughnessy, Mina P. "Diving In: An Introduction to Basic Writing." *College Composition and Communication* 27 (1976): 234–39.

———. *Errors and Expectations: A Guide for the Teacher of Basic Writing*. New York: Oxford University Press, 1977.

Sommers, Nancy. "Responding to Student Writing." *College Composition and Communication* 33 (1982): 148–56.

Soven, Margot Iris. *Teaching Writing in Middle and Secondary Schools: Theory, Research, and Practice.* Boston: Allyn and Bacon, 1995.

Straub, Richard, and Ronald F. Lunsford. *Twelve Readers Reading.* Cresskill, NJ: Hampton Press, 1995.

CHAPTER 10

Rethinking Ways to Teach Young Writers: Response and Evaluation in the Creative Writing Course

Stephanie Vanderslice

Having someone read my work was terrifying, and the thought of their [*sic*] response was almost enough to make me bolt through the closest escape route.

—Brandi

Before this class, I must admit, I was terrified of allowing others to read anything I'd written.

—Jill

It's so much like exposing your soul—laying everything wide open for all to see and criticize.

—Lori

In their dramatic effect, these respective quotes from Brandi, Jill, and Lori exemplify the feelings of many students in my introductory creative writing courses. Most of these are students who have some confidence in themselves as writers who presumably like to write and who have chosen this class to seek new ways to improve their writing further. Yet, their trepidation is palpable, for creative writing courses have traditionally gained a reputation as being a rather harsh breeding ground, where inexperienced writers may "sink or swim" according to the teacher's perceived merits of their work. Indeed, many of these courses have been led by teachers whose great passion lies in a text outside the classroom and who may be diffident at best and caustic at worst.[1] It is no wonder then that students harbor some fear; they are just discovering their voices, sending out tentative textual roots in an atmosphere where the goal, more than in a composition or technical writing class, is often, according to Wendy Bishop, to separate the "wheat from the chaff"; the "real writer" from the "dilletantes" (*Released* 158). They have then found themselves in an atmosphere that creates, according to Hans Ostrum, an "economy of scarcity," where just one or two students may be singled out as "stars" (166).

Many factors contribute to this economy. Certainly, the professor, whose mind may be more on the manuscript in his or her study than the one in the classroom, is a contributory factor. Yet, the majority of instructors are well-intentioned teacher-writers. Perhaps the most responsible factor is the perception that creative writing is "different" from texts written in other classes, an explanation frequently invoked in order to allow it to be taught in a social and pedagogical "vacuum" (Bishop, *Released* 158). Thus, many such classes are still taught using the "workshop method" that originated a half-century ago at the prestigious Iowa Fiction Workshops, a conventional "apprenticeship-model" that posits the teacher as gatekeeper, or, according to Patrick Bizarro, the "exemplary reader" whom the novice writer aims to please (240). Within this vacuum, many instructors find it easy to "finesse" the issue of responding to, commenting on, or grading student work with a figurative "throwing up of the hands," a metaphorical "it cannot be done" that is based upon the idea that creative work is too subjective to be objectively evaluated (Bishop, *Released* 157). As Bishop suggests in "Responding to Creative Writing," the shortfall of this attitude is that it rationalizes its practitioners' return to "canon formation . . . technique . . . and craft" and away from pedagogical issues of response and evaluation, which, to varying degrees, occupy their counterparts in closely allied fields such as composition and literature (180).

In his essay "Reading the Creative Writing Course," Patrick Bizarro argues persuasively that what the traditional model of tradition and textual commentary is particularly guilty of is its neglect of student needs. The approach leads teachers to do little more than "appropriate" student work and take authority away from those who created it. Moreover, such an appropriation often occurs in service to what compositionists Lil Brannon and C.H. Knoblauch describe in their article "On Students' Rights," one of the earliest treatises on teacher response, as the "Ideal Text," a reader-driven image of what the "developing text ought to look like or ought to be doing" (118). According to Brannon and Knoblauch, when teachers respond to emergent student writing, whether in composition or creative writing, using the "Ideal Text" model, the kind of appropriation that occurs distracts from what a writer was "attempting to do" in achieving his or her own purposes. Furthermore, a chief limitation of the "Ideal Text," they argue, is that it "compromises" the teacher's "ability to help students say effectively what they truly want to say" (119).

Nancy Sommers confirms in another landmark study, "Responding to Student Writing," that even the most well-meaning teachers using the "Ideal Text" model tend "not to respond to student writing with the kind of thoughtful commentary which will help [students] think about their purposes and goals in writing a specific text" (107). This is why, as an alternative, Sommers proposes "comment on student writing to dramatize the presence of a reader to help our students become the questioning reader themselves" (107).

The point I want to add is that tutoring the young writer to become "the questioning reader" is a goal I stress in my creative writing course, where I strive to convey to students that the creative and critical abilities are two sides of the same coin. To the realization of this objective I consider teacher commentary and response essential. Many students come to my creative writing classes as "competent" writers in the most abstract sense of the word; most are at wildly variant stages of their development as poets, fiction writers, essayists, or dramatists. To apply a universal "Ideal Text" to students at such disparate points along this continuum seems arbitrary at best and certainly not in the optimum interests of their development as writers. Yet, when it comes to their ability to critically examine their own texts and those of others, most students stand together at a common starting point—as novices. Nonetheless, as many creative writing teachers will attest at least anecdotally, under the right conditions, critical ability often develops at a faster pace than creative ability, that is, students often learn to speak and write quite eloquently of the strengths and weaknesses of a given piece of writing well before they may be able to create similarly effective creative texts. Nothwithstanding, their eventual achievement of this "next step" in their development as creative writers is often the direct result of their burgeoning critical skills.

Consequently, in revising my course, I turned away from the conventional product-based workshop focused on response to and evaluation of nearly "final" drafts and toward a process-oriented approach that responded to student work as drafts in progress. Fundamental to this shift was also a change in evaluative focus that revolutionized the way I responded to my students' work: I stopped grading their creative efforts. This is not to say that my students were not evaluated over the course of the semester—they were, repeatedly—or that I resorted to the same "throwing up of hands" as my peers. Instead, students were graded, indeed rather sternly, on assignments that encouraged their development as readers and critics, instruments that I will describe later in this essay. I stopped grading my students' creative work but continued responding to it.

This simple but monumental change altered the nature of my commentary and the students' reaction to it.

As I tried to get past the grade, one of my students reacted by writing as follows:

I'll never forget the anger that welled in my belly and the blood that rushed to my face when I received that paper back, that paper which I perceived to be one of my best, and saw where the instructor had written "So" out beside one of my sentences. So? can you believe that?

—Natalie

I could not recall having made such a marginal comment on any student's paper. But in assessing my students' work I have often struggled with the notion that, by scrawling a C+ on a piece a student had slaved over, I was doing just that, essentially boiling what may have been a half-page of written summary and a half dozen margin notes to: "So? Is this the best you can do?" Consequently, as many of my creative writing colleagues admit to doing,[2] I tended then to inflate students' grades, giving some a higher grade than they deserved, grading effort rather than the quality of the work.

Looking back, I think I did this for two reasons: first, in order to encourage the student to keep writing, and second, but perhaps more importantly, to direct the student's attention more to my commentary and less to the grade. I came to realize that nothing, however, achieved both of these goals with quite the same effectiveness as surrendering the grade altogether. Suddenly, my comments became meaningful in and of themselves, rather than as explanations of a grade. In doing so, they took on an entirely new dimension, something the students responded to immediately, as reactions such as the following testify:

In a field as subjective as creative writing, it is easy to say if I get a bad grade on something—then, of course—you must have hated it on a personal level and you just didn't "get it." I don't think this will get anybody very far. In some ways, only having your comments was a less harsh way to say, "I think this needs some work" rather than "I think this needs some work: 'F.'" And it is hard to distinguish whether or not the piece you'd like to give an 'F' to was thrown together last night and deserves an 'F' or if it was a genuine and sincere effort, because I don't think anyone would want to give a genuine and sincere effort an 'F.'

—Sarah

Once I got my first response back, all my fear diminished. The comments I received were objective and encouraging. I liked the fact that my works themselves were not graded. It is hard to stomach a B when you think your paper deserved an A, especially with creative writing. A lot more of the soul goes into writing a story or poem than it does into a research paper on popcorn.

—Brandi

Aside from the wave of assent of this kind that rippled through my classes, responding without the onus of a grade achieved something else: It freed me at last to consider a student's work on its own terms rather than comparing it to that of another student or worse yet, holding it up to the "Ideal Text."

I could focus on what was working in a poem or story and encourage a student to expand on that without worrying about how such encouragement might lead that same student to expect a higher grade than he or she would actually receive. In terms of commentary, I have often found that focusing on what works in a piece of creative writing, what the student is doing well, is often a good way to infer an author's intentions regarding a piece. Without the pressure of a grade, moreover, I was finally free to let my true instincts as a responder come through, to overcome the tendency to put on my "exemplary reader" spectacles for the purpose of evaluation. Indeed, I was able to respond as an explorer discovering the author in a text, suggesting ways that the author might make his or her intentions more visible. In characterizing this kind of response, the following description by one of my students is perhaps more effective than any I could come up with:

I appreciate how you gave us specific examples of, say, dialogue that was well done. . . . Your criticisms always seemed to be given in a protective shell that said to the writer, 'you did a very good job, let's see how we can make this better. . . . It wasn't cutting and accusatory but helpful.

—Sarah

Despite the level of success that I have obtained in my use of this alternative method of student assessment, I haven't "gone soft" in leading students to become better readers of their own work. How then do I justify this "no grading policy"? The short answer is that the creative work students hand in is about the only writing they are not graded on over the course of the semester. Complementing this work, I have created two additional assignment categories that are graded and heavily weighted—cover letters and responses. Both of these categories were calibrated specifically to complement and support my comments.

Each creative piece my students hand in is required to have a one- to two-page cover letter attached to it in which they describe to me the process of writing it, specifically discussing problems they encountered, responses to peer critique, perceived strengths and weaknesses, and, most critically, the kind of feedback they are looking for. Modified from Wendy Bishop's "Executive Summary" ("Responding to Creative Writing" 186), the purpose of this cover letter is twofold. First, and perhaps foremost, it gives me an insight into the writer's work that I would not ordinarily receive, insight that can direct my response more effectively than anything else.

For example, if Ross turns in three poems, one of which is a four-line verse on the merits of a bug zapper, but tells me in his cover letter that he worked hard on the poem about his grandfather's death and included the bug zapper poems because he thought I'd get a kick out of it, I learn where my response efforts will be best spent. Further, if he tells me he's really worried about whether his poem to his brother sounds "cheesy" I can hone in on the sentimental aspects of the piece.

Second, writing about their own works gives emerging authors practice in reading and analyzing it, moving them one step closer to becoming their own best readers. As further incentive to the students, all of these cover letters are carefully graded for thoughtfulness, insight, attention to detail, critical effort, and presentation. To assist them, at the beginning of the semester, I hand out copies of successful and unsuccessful cover letters from past courses to give the students an idea of what I expect. Cover letters, then, enhance my own written comments and at the same time encourage the kind of "writer autonomy, authority, and ownership of a text" proposed by Bishop ("Responding to Creative Writing" 186).

The response paper is the other central component of the course designed to enhance students' critical abilities. Over the course of the semester, each student experiences what I call a "full class workshop," where his or her work is critiqued by the class as a whole. The week before, the student-author distributes copies of this work to the class. Each class member is then responsible for coming to the subsequent full-class workshop with two copies of a typed critique discussing the student-author's work—one which they hand in to the author and another that they hand in to me. I grade each response paper for depth and detail. Combined, the average of what amounts to roughly 20 response papers equals about one-third of the student's grade that semester.

To give the students practice, I discount the grade on the first two responses but comment on them to suggest means of improvement. For example, if a student writes a brief response telling me "I loved Emily's story. I can't think of anything wrong with it," I ask for elaboration: "Can you be more specific? What did you like about it?" In addition, at the end of the semester, students are required to put two responses in their course portfolio: the most helpful response they received, along with a written explanation of why it was helpful, and the most helpful response they wrote with a similar explanation. Making these response papers count so highly forces the students to take them more seriously than they otherwise would. It was surely by heavily weighing these two assignments that I was able to avoid the kinds of grade inflation that might plague a "subjective" course such as creative writing. I could concentrate on improving the focus of my own response, the feedback the student-authors received from their peers, and the class discussions that took place in full-class workshops.

Hans Ostrum suggests that writing classes endeavor to counter the "economy of scarcity" with what he calls an "economy of abundance, in which every student is an explorer of language, literature, memory, the social construction of literary standards, authorship . . . meaning, and so forth, an economy in which students' texts are less 'commodities' that need to be 'priced' . . . and more a means of discovery" (167). Ostrum's dictum offers an admirable vista that I strive to explore in reconfiguring my creative writing classes. To make the classroom more liberatory, more authority is released to students.

I should like to conclude this study by relating one event that indicates to me that some of the strategies taught in my creative writing classes are being used beyond the classroom in the writing world. During a recent layover in the Memphis airport, I met a young woman traveling with her toddler son. We chatted briefly and, when my occupation came up, the woman mentioned that she had developed a new-found interest in writing during a difficult period in her life. While her daughter was ill, she wrote letters to family members describing the ups and downs of her progress. "It wasn't the kind of writing I did in college," she explained. "It was different. People in my family told me I was good at writing about what was happening. Now I'm glad I have the letters, as a record of that time." As our conversation continued, it became clear that the woman had, in fact, lost her daughter to a debilitating illness.

That it should take a tragic event for this woman to come to know the power of writing did not come to me as a surprise. In *Bird By Bird: Some Instructions on Writing and Life*, a book I often assign to my students, Anne Lammot writes of this power of writing for its therapeutic end rather than for the glory of "publication": "[T]here is still something to be said for painting portraits of the people we have loved, for trying to express those moments that seem inexpressibly beautiful, the ones that change us and deepen us" (192). Writing that is not abstract but memorial is not only critical to efforts to transform private subjec- tivities into history or communal experiences, it holds an important place in our human efforts to keep our sense of the past preserved. This is why memorial writing can play such a central role in leading survivors in the journey toward recovery. Within this frame of creativity, then, students must be encouraged, as Lee Martin maintains, to use writing to develop the reflective, critical skills without which they cannot hope to be able to truthfully examine and represent their worlds (179).

NOTES

1. Certainly this "archetype" is beginning to change as forces in creative writing and composition, led by Bishop, Ostrum, and others, validate the teaching of creative writing in the profession. Nonetheless, it is historically accurate.

2. In fact, it is not uncommon for the final grade rosters of many creative writing classes to be dominated by A's with only the occasional B or lower grades for students whose lack of effort in the course is all too obvious. But for so long as the practice of grade inflation remains prevalent in evaluations of creative writing, for so long will it devalue the courses in the academy.

WORKS CITED

Bishop, Wendy. *Released into Language: Options for Teaching Creative Writing.* 2nd ed. Portland, ME: Calendar Islands, 1998.

————. "Responding to Creative Writing: Students as Teachers and the Executive Summary." In *Teaching Writing Creatively*, edited by David Starkey, 180–86. Portsmouth, NH: Heinemann, Boynton, Cook, 1998.

Bizarro, Patrick. "Reading the Creative Writing Course: The Teacher's Many Selves." In *Colors of a Different Horse: Rethinking Creative Writing Theory and Pedagogy*, edited by Wendy Bishop and Hans Ostrum, 234–47. Urbana, IL: NCTE, 1994.

Brannon, Lil, and C.H. Knoblauch. "On Students' Rights to their Own Texts: A Model of Teacher Response." In *A Sourcebook for Student Writing*, edited by Richard Straub, 117–28. Cresskill, NJ: Hampton Press, 1999.

Lamott, Anne. *Bird by Bird: Some Instructions on Writing and Life.* New York: Anchor-Doubleday, 1994.

Martin, Lee. "My Other, My Self: Participants and Spectators in 'Introductory' Fiction Writing Workshops." In *Teaching Writing Creatively*, edited by David Starkey, 172–79. Portsmouth, NH: Heinemann, Boynton, Cook, 1998.

Ostrum, Hans. " 'Carom Shots': Reconceptualizing Imitation and Its Uses in Creative Writing Courses." In *Teaching Writing Creatively*, edited by David Starkey. Portsmouth, NH: Heinemann, Boynton, Cook, 1998.

Sommers, Nancy. "Responding to Student Writing." In *A Sourcebook for Responding to Student Writing*, edited by Richard Straub, 107–116. Cresskill, NJ: Hampton Press, 1999.

CHAPTER 11

From Commentary to Conference
Margaret Christian

Although my primary specialty is sixteenth-century English literature, I've taught several composition classes, overwhelmingly classes of freshmen, each year during the last decade. In that time, I've become much less interested in grading student papers and justifying those grades with my comments, than in teaching—and particularly, in providing feedback as to "how this strikes the reader" and offering suggestions for revision. My interest is at odds with the students' preoccupation with that grade (and their tendency to personalize both grades and comments), so I've developed my response to student papers as a way of redirecting the student writer's interest away from both the personal and the grade. I want them to care about what I care about: How will a reader respond to this piece of writing? How can it be better? I've found three strategies particularly helpful: limiting topics, "magnetic conferencing" or responding to papers via cassette tape, and using a seminar format for peer revision conferences.

The easiest first step that I take in keeping commentary from being interpreted personally is to limit the paper topics to those that lend themselves to objective discussion. What topics are out of bounds under this rule must depend to some extent on the teacher as well as on the student. The thumb rule is this: If I take offense at something in the paper, I may grade it unfairly; if a student opens too delicate a topic, the most gently worded suggestion may sound brutal. For example, once a nontraditional student of mine handed in a "how to" paper detailing his experience beating a drunk driving rap. The paper was pretty good from a formal standpoint, for it contained a riveting narrative, vivid descriptive passages, accurate word choice, full paragraph development, coherence, and an acceptable level of grammatical accuracy. However, it left a lot to be desired in terms of addressing the rhetorical situation with a sense of moral probity. I could probably offer dispassionate feedback on such a paper on the basis of its rhetoric now, but at that time I graded it (probably too generously) in a misery of rage and self-mistrust. As a consequence, I was denied the ability to summon enough impulse and patience to offer the student the kind of detailed comments that could have challenged him to rethink and refine his presentation.

On another occasion, a provisional student submitted a mechanically—and grammatically—challenged personal narrative on his girlfriend's pregnancy, taking the reader through her announcement, his urging her to have an abortion, her reluctance, his breaking up with her, and her getting the abortion. It seemed that for my student the memory was such a searing indictment of his human failure that it proved useless as an occasion to improve his writing. Not only did it seem that the faults in his paper and the faults in his behavior were indistinguishable in his mind, it appeared that the wound was there before I could make any comment.

Of course, some students have been able to accept constructive advice, and to even hold rational class discussions, about papers featuring personal or controversial topics such as unplanned pregnancies, dying grandparents, shoplifting arrests, and other problems. The difficulty arises only when the writer is unable to take the subject beyond the level of sensationalism. A student writer who is inordinately preoccupied to satisfy these lower appetites is more likely to fail in his or her paper to broaden and deepen and sharpen awareness of life. When the student writer fails to provide any revealing insights about fundamental human problems, he or she is guilty of superficial treatment of the subject. Thus, I have often told my students right from the first or second day of class, "Don't tell/write anything about yourself in a paper that you would be ashamed for your favorite grandmother to know, unless you redeem the situation by getting punished or doing the right thing. If you commit a crime or hurt somebody else in a paper, be sure to either get caught or learn from it, preferably both."

Having decided on these rather ethically rigorous measures, I may have prevented my students from writing some very entertaining papers that might, ultimately, have led to unhelpful emotional exposure on my part as well as on the part of the student writers. But whatever the negative effect of such imposed limitation, it is more than compensated for by the fact that it fosters more objectivity than otherwise would be the case in giving the students feedback. Inevitably, I want students to know that for literary writing to have compelling claim on the reader's attention, it must offer more than escape; it must go beyond the terrain of the soap opera. Thus, to further minimize the opportunity for the students to recount personal experiences in a lazy and unethical manner, I often encourage them to stick to topics that require additional research, and I offer them detailed advice on how they can impose sensibility on their stories.

When I use the cassette tape method, the goal remains the same: to allow the students to focus on how their paper comes across and how it can be improved—as opposed to taking comments personally or focusing exclusively on the grade. To help me offer comments on cassette tape, I carefully read through the paper underlining, circling, inserting carats, or scribbling abbreviations that will aid me in remembering the points that I wish to stress. I talk about the paper to the cassette tape recorder as if I were having a conference with the student writer. I open with an assessment of what the paper seems to accomplish, then talk generally about where I see the paper going, and what I would aim for in revision if it were my paper. I say something like "Let's go through the paper together and I'll tell you what I mean." As I talk locally about the sentences or paragraphs—an interesting idea at number one that needs development, a lack of evidence at number two, a confusing citation, a felicitous word choice, an elegantly worded or awkward phrase ("This way of putting it doesn't fit; how would so and so work, instead?")—I write the numbers on the paper to code my comments on the tape.

Writing clearly, I try to offer alternative ways to word a sentence and suggestions on fleshing out an idea rather than just writing "awkward" or "develop this thought." It takes very little time to say, "Here, at number four, are two complete sentences that are joined with nothing but a comma; that's a serious mistake. There are several more of them in the paper, though I've only marked this one." Students have told me that they find such comments a lot more understandable than "cs" (or even "comma splice") scribbled in the margin of their papers.[1] The strategy also allows me to take the time to acknowledge the good intent behind a problematic rhetorical choice.

If a student writes about how to "sanctify the goldfish bowl," as a colleague's student once did, I could say, "I notice that you are are varying your word choice, and I want you to keep experimenting. Try to be really hard on yourself at the same time, though; I think if you read this phrase aloud in the process of writing, you will find that it doesn't sound quite right to you, either. Keep the thesaurus handy, but make sure you choose a word that will work in this context."

Though students may think otherwise, one of the good things about the "magnetic conference" mode of teacher commentary is that there's no grade on the paper. If students do not listen to the tape, they have no way of knowing how I judged their work. I want to emphasize the paper's effect on a reader and its possibilities for revision, so I have decided to not assign even tentative grades. It is so easy for students to mistake the teacher's expressed excitement and optimism about a paper's prospect for revision; they often take that as enthusiasm about the actual draft they had handed in and, accordingly, devote less attention to revising. To forestall such an outcome, at the end of a recorded comment, I'll say something like "If I were assigning this paper a grade right now, it wouldn't pass. It is really important that the paper provide more examples/acknowledge and answer the opposing point of view/document its sources in the correct format/be absolutely free from serious errors of sentence structure, like comma splices and fragments."

When a student has managed to put a stronger draft together, it's time for more enthusiastic response. On a recent paper on binge drinking among college students, for instance, I wrote as follows: "You are off to a good start. In fact, this paper would already earn a passing grade, but if you'd like to improve it to the level of a B, you might want to strengthen the argument, perhaps by adding further examples, from actual campuses, of each of the general points you make about alcoholism among college students. Beyond that, you might want to try a more arresting technique in the introduction that could add some polish and interest to your paper and raise the eventual grade even higher."

While striving to be specific without being intimidating or discouraging, taped comments can put a humane touch on teacher commentary without sacrificing candidness. This is why, in the event, for example, that a student turns in a "revision" that fails to incorporate any previous suggestions, I can relieve my feelings and still not create a barrier between myself and the student if I say, "This version does not reflect the concerns that I mentioned on the tape last time. I'm sure you listened to the whole tape, so I won't record over that last message any further."

Let me return to the issue of the seminar as a format for peer revision. I might have hinted that it is strategy that has worked better for me than the small, informal revision groups I used to divide the class into for discussing drafts of student papers.[2] Three days before the day the peer revision conference is scheduled to be held, those students whose works will be featured (usually two in a 50-minute period) distribute copies of their paper to every class member. On the day of the presentation, the assigned discussants (one per paper) distribute copies of a discussion guide to each class member.[3]

The discussion guide, typed on one single-spaced sheet, is divided into three parts to permit orderly presentation. The first part, devoted to "Summary," outlines the main arguments of the paper; the second, "Commenting and Analysis," details the paper's rhetoric, the method of its argument; while the last part, "Questions for Discussion," raises at least four key problems related to the paper for discussion. I ensure good management of the 25 minutes to be devoted by the class to each paper. Thus, following the main presentation by each speaker, the class offers time for any other comments that class members wish to make before I close with concluding remarks.

Although the major responsibility for providing discussion guides rests with each student writer, I try to spice up the learning as much as I can with humor, and I offer advice on organizational matters as well. The goal is not only to allow students as much productive creative freedom as possible, but also to pry open critical insights that might otherwise remain hidden to them. The task of rhetorical analysis is new to most freshmen, and many need a lot of individual instruction to differentiate summarizing content from critical commentary on matters such as structure and style. Nor are many of them comfortable determining a writer's purpose and persuasively judging whether it was achieved.

It is so easy for students to fall into the habit of plot summarizing; the task of thinking up good questions is a challenge I help students to overcome. I find that making students write and revise their discussion guides and making them listen to and participate in discussions about their classmates' papers, position them in a much better state where they are equipped to notice things in their own writing and to know the various alternative ways open to them for getting their ideas across.[4]

There are a variety of objectives that composition teachers can lay claims to. My own goal, put quite simply, is to help student writers become better readers of their own writing and then to know how to improve the things in their papers that don't work well. To do this, I encourage them to avoid topics that are too emotionally fraught to lend themselves to clear treatment. Student writers need to face all of the travails of writing. I have found the use of tape-recorded comments and the seminar conference to be the best ways of offering guidance to student writers. Through these methods, I am able to immerse students more thoroughly into the practice of rhetorical analysis and creative thinking by moving them from being passive recipients of the teacher's lessons into being active participants—as presenters, discussants, and respondents in a small, controlled, but genuinely serious writers' conference.

NOTES

1. Since I do not devote class time to teaching standard grammar, punctuation, or syntax, I follow up with sheets directing individual students to the appropriate sections of the handbook and requiring an appointment at the writing center to review the issues both in the handbook and in their papers.

2. I have adapted this idea from a method spelled out by John N. King in his 1999 National Endowment for the Humanities (NEH) Summer Seminar "The English Reformation: History, Literature, and Art," held at Ohio State University. John's watchword, "I like a seminar that generates a lot of paper," was put into action with his insistence that every participant-led discussion feature a handout.

3. Each student is also required to read the papers ahead of time and write a paragraph or two of reaction and suggestions for revision.

4. Taken as a group, the three discussion guides, each of which goes through a revision process and is graded, count as one of the six required "major writing assignments" in Pennsylvannia State University's English 15 class.

CHAPTER 12

Moving Students beyond Defensiveness and Anxiety in Writing Assignments

Thomas Earl Midgette

In this chapter, I approach the topic of teacher commentary from the vantage point of graduate-level instruction, in a department (educational psychology) where each student is expected to "write across the curriculum." At least in principle, though less in practice, we expect students to write papers in their discipline and related courses—with some professors requiring 15- to 20-page research papers examining some topic related to counseling or the helping profession. Typically a list of topics, each of which is related to the professor's reseach interest and consistent with the course being taught, is provided to the student by the professor. After the sudents have completed the research paper, each one of them presents it in a classroom setting, in a forum that is a simulation of a conference format. In this presentation, the student-presenter provides a five-page written handout that includes (a) title page, (b) abstract, (c) introduction and thesis, (d) major findings, and (e) conclusion and references.

As any concerned teacher will bear out, a good way to bring about qualitative improvement in student writing is for the student and the professor to be intricately involved from the beginning of the written assignment. An assignment is made with expectations related to a specific topic and its length and format. When the student's written assignment is analyzed and critiqued, the instructor considers it in its various stages of development, including draft and thematic formulation, formation, rewrites, finalization, presentation, and reporting. In finally grading the assignment, the professor passes judgment on the form, function, effort, and the overall quality of the work. The instructor's response to student output is thus usually given in order to improve the clarity and the breadth, as well as the depth of the research, in alignment with the instructor's disciplinary framework.

Anyone who has tried this mode knows that the simulated presentation allows the student to tap from the professor's experience and much more. Following the performance, the simulated presentation enables the student presenter to learn as much from the questions raised by the presenter's classmates about the different aspects of the paper as he or she learns from the instructor. When students opt to complete the written assignment with two or three other students, the activity reflects a group project. In all circumstances, the research is conducted under an approved documentation style, such as American Psychological Association (APA), under the supervision of a committee of three faculty. It is vital that the students understand and master practical and theoretical writing matters and that the use of technology is encouraged. We realize that the professor can either facilitate learning or exacerbate the student's anxiety or "phobic" reactions about writing assignments.

Writing is a creative, analytical, subjective, cultural, aesthetic process, which gives hope to the hopeless and a voice to the voiceless. An existential exercise, it cannot be separated from one's concept of self. If we hold such a view of writing, I believe we can find some high ground for joining writing instruction and Paulo Freire's view of education. In *Pedagogy of Hope*, Freire defines education as an activity that is by its very nature "directive (creative) and political" (78). Yet, to him, the best way to teach is to allow educands "to defend a thesis, a position, a preference with earnestness, defend it rigorously but passionately and at the same time stimulate the contrary discourse" (78). The best teacher, in Freire's estimation, therefore, respects educands' "right to utter" a "discourse" of their choice (78).

Freire recognizes that "educational practice" is, inevitably, "always directive" but warns that the moment the educator "directivity" interferes with the creative, formulative, and investigative capacity of the educand, then, "directivity is transformed into manipulation and authoritarianism" (79). The tasks of "the progressive educator," Freire believes, are to use "a serious, correct political analysis . . . to unveil opportunities for hope, no matter what the obstacles may be" (133). Freire defines writing as an act of learning in which students, to a degree, work from their own understanding of their place in history, politics, and social bearing. Since writing is an important "extension of the struggle to thwart injustices," Freire warns that it is "impermissible to educate without an understanding of how society works" (133).

What about the views of W. Purkey and J. Novak? They identify what they call "inviting" and "disinviting" verbal comments, personal behaviors, and physical environments used by educators to facilitate or thwart student writing. Among the positive strategies they recommend are the following:

a. holding positive and high expectations for students and their work

b. respecting the individual uniqueness of each student

c. establishing cooperative relationships with students

d. fostering encouraging environment and relations with and among student learners

e. establishing good human relations with students

f. being inviting toward students

g. putting the student at the center of the learning process. (2–20)

Ten years earlier, W. Bernard and W. Huckins expressed similar ideas, outlining several propositions needed in the classroom to facilitate learning. As they, too, emphasize, only when the teacher creates an enabling environment can students be expected to work well. Today, their list still holds true, especially their argument that students will learn more

a. when their innate curiosity and their urge to explore, to grow, to experience, to become, and cope with their environment are nurtured by the teacher

b. when the student's total personality is considered, and the teacher does not attempt to isolate the cognitive from the affective

c. when the uniqueness of each student's learning skill potentials, styles, and learning modes is recognized by the teacher

d. when there is a recognition of the relationship between self-concepts, readiness, and aspiration to learn

e. when the teacher recognizes the centrality of the ego-concept

f. when the teacher utilizes the self-concept paradigm to optimize instruction in a milieu that takes into account that self-concepts are socially determined

g. when the teacher regards the writing process as more important than the product itself

h. when the teacher is perceived as a model who engages in writing and scholarly activities him/herself

i. when students work together with their peers in writing and researching. (23)

Perhaps, no one can put all of this in more fitting terms than C.H. Patterson, who has defined learning as a collaborative activity. Since "the teacher can only create the positive conditions for learning," the best teaching, Patterson believes, is that which, "through establishing a personal relation, frees the student to learn" (98).

What are the lessons that I draw from these ideas? My first rule of thumb is that only when appropriate strategies are employed can students be brought to their highest level of educational performance. With respect to writing, the educational philosophy of the teacher is critical—more so in a situation with multicultural implications. Here, both the students and the instructor bring their racial, cultural, and ethnic differences to the writing experience. Irrespective of the academic levels of the students, writing should be approached as a creative experience that takes account of the cultural background of both the students and their instructor.

Not only are culturally determined characteristics brought to the classroom to shape the human dynamics of the writing experience, but a student's every activity in and around the classroom—pedagogical, extracurricular, and social—is deeply affected by his or her own cultural background. A number of variables may cause student and professor to encounter cultural conflicts that hinder the transmission of cognitive and/or instructional knowledge. For example, the cognitive categories of the student may not match those of the professor, and each party may be familiar with some features of reality unknown to the other. In other words, student and professor may experience a misalignment of cognitive maps.

There could also be a case in which the personal relationship between student and professor becomes undermined by culturally based misunderstandings and divergent expectations that destroy efforts to build a positive atmosphere that would be conducive to learning. When the process by which the professor expects the student to learn is considerably different from the one by which the student has learned to write within his or her own culture, this can present an area of difficulty as problematic as when student and professor hold different motivations for the writing assignment and the process.

I want to argue that a good writing instructor makes the writing experience, as well as the classroom, a space for open, genuine, and creative encounters for positive human interactions and exchange of ideas. Such a teacher recognizes the uniqueness of the learner and confirms that learner's person as an individual and a linked member of the global community. There can be a disconnect between professor and student, resulting from their holding varying levels of commitment to scholarship and liberatory education and change and from their different abilities to both ask the "pertinent" questions and answer them. So, we cannot ignore the issue of student/professor situatedness. This is all to say that the levels of content/discontent that student and professor have with the status quo must be taken into account.

All too often, students are simply writing to meet the professor's expectations or to satisfy the course requirements. They seem to be less interested in liberatory education or engaged pedagogy for the practice of freedom. But if writing is, as bell hooks argues, an act by means of which students can be engaged in a conversation or dialogical education, then, the instructor should play the part of the artist and politician engaging students in cultural action in and outside the classroom. Writing assignments and papers should drive students and professors toward answers for questions through a pedagogy that enables the examination of societal ills that could ultimately lead to social empowerment.

bell hooks's counsel, that writing and teaching be practiced within an ambience of radical ideas, carries implications with which I concur: writing ought to be liberatory, serving the multiple purposes of enlightening both the writer and the discipline. I accept hooks's contention that the instructor acknowledge and value each student's presence and being and that teaching serve as a performative act though which voice and dialog are engaged by writing. hooks is right: Engaged pedagogy respects and cares for the soul, for actualization and for the process of expression. A transformative act, writing should not only move the writer away from the oppressor's language but also confront race, gender, and class in its quest to tame injustice (203).

As a coda to hooks's wisdom, one would have to return to Paulo Freire's judgment: "[D]ialogue between teacher and student does not place them on the same footing . . . but it does mark the democratic position between them . . . dialogue does not level them . . . [and it is] not a favor done by one for the other . . . [it only] implies a sincere, fundamental respect by student and professor" (116–17). As could be expected, it is to promote freedom of expression by enabling students to explore their intellectual interests in a manner rooted in mutual respect that my comments are framed in a clear, timely, and generous spirit. The main types of comments that I provide students with can be classified under the following categories:

1. Those that stress the need to explain a paper's thesis more clearly. (Comments of this sort are made where a paper's main point lies buried, making further clarification a requirement.)

2. Those that relate the need to align the material reported in a paper with the title. (Observations of this nature are pertinent where a paper's title is not congruent with what is discussed within its pages.)

3. Comments that ask the student to shorten a paper's paragraphs. (Such statements follow where paragraphs are too long; for example, where one paragraph includes several unrelated themes/ideas.)

4. Comments that indicate a need to update a paper's references. (This is mandatory when secondary sources are outdated, usually when the most current citation is more than 10 years old.)

5. Comments that require a student to develop a paper's paragraphs more fully. (This type of suggestion is appropriate when information is missing within a paper's paragraphs.)

6. Comments that point out the importance of a paper's topic of discussion, but which advise the student to not assume this to be self-evident. (Such comments are useful when a student needs to state his or her topic's significance more clearly because a thesis statement is absent in the paper.)

7. Comments that ask the student to support his or her claims with concrete details/examples. (This sort of advice is given when the discussion is vague or incoherent or rambling or unfocused.)

8. Statements that mandate the student to make a push for the final thrust of a paper. (This kind of directive is made when the argument of a paper requires synthesis; where the implications of the research are not clearly made manifest.)

9. Comments that discourage making sweeping generalizations. (With these I indicate where in the paper exceptional cases are used as bases for running commentary or where fallacious reasoning occurs.)

10. Comments that address the issue of whether or not a bibliographic format has been followed accurately.

Even though the majority of the students who write for me are working in a nonliterary field, I take the time to encourage them to be sensitive to style, to savor the fruits of good writing, to regard style as a labor of love. Often writing is a challenge for many students. Although some have benefited from English Composition at some point in their education, many others have tended to be overwhelmed both by writing and the teacher's comments relating to it. While some students take on the challenge posed by teacher commentary, some are devasted and frozen by it. Less prepared students flounder and turn in the same drafts with few changes. For the most part, however, when my marginal notes seem to have provided too little information for students to make constructive changes in their written assignments, I have tried to alleviate their level of anxiety and defensiveness by expanding the range of my commentary through conversations held in one-on-one conferences with students. In my commentary, I focus on both content and style because I believe that the two cannot be separated. Rather than focus on a single issue, I approach student writing on many fronts. Instead of expending energy and passion criticizing, I show how flaws can be removed. Similarly, without wishing to give my ideas the status of sacrosanct truths, I believe they are open-ended enough to be helpful to student writers attempting to revise their work.

WORKS CITED

Bernard, W.H. and W.C. Huckins. *Humanism in the Classroom: An Eclectic Approach to Teaching and Learning.* Boston: Allyn and Bacon, 1974.

Freire, P. *Pedagogy of Hope.* New York: Continuum Publishing, 1994.

Hanna, F.J., W.B. Talley, and M.H. Guindon. "The Power of Perception: Toward a Model of Cultural Oppression and Liberation. " *Journal of Counseling and Development* 78 (2000): 430–41.

hooks, b. *Teaching to Transgress: Education as the Practice of Freedom.* New York: Routledge, 1994.

Patterson, C.H. *Humanistic Education.* Englewood Cliffs, NJ: Prentice-Hall, 1973.

Purkey, W.J., and J.M. Novak. *Inviting Success: A Self-Concept Approach to Teaching and Learning.* Belmont, CA: Wadsworth Publishing, 1984.

Shor, I., and P. Freire. *A Pedagogy for Liberation: Dialogues on Transformative Education.* New York: Bergin and Garvey, 1987.

CHAPTER 13

Rigor, Rigor, Rigor, the Rigor of Death: A Dose of Discipline Shot through Teacher Response to Student Writing

Ode Ogede

Richard Straub, in a remarkable essay explaining the different implications of a variety of forms in which teacher response to student writing has traditionally been expressed, writes as follows:

> [T]he more comments a teacher makes on a piece of writing, the more controlling he will likely be. The more a teacher attends to the text, especially local matters, and tries to lead the student to produce a more complete written product, the more likely he is to point to specific changes and the more he is likely to exert over the student's writing. The more a teacher attends to the student's writing processes and the larger contexts of writing, and gears his comments to the student behind the text and her ongoing work as a writer, the less likely he is to point to specific changes and the less control he is likely to assume over the student's writing. (*Sourcebook* 134–35)

The question of which approach to adopt in responding to student writing becomes a highly charged one for us as instructors because we know from experience that in and out of the classroom we deal with students who have come from different backgrounds and who have learned to react in different ways to efforts to educate them. Moreover, as teachers, our good intentions can be misinterpreted. Without debating which of the various models of instructor response to student writing is inherently superior, a sign that should dictate each choice an instructor makes is the specific class context and student composition. Whereas a *laissez faire* climate might work well in writing classes with fairly sophisticated student writers, what goes on in the other types of writing classes predominantly made up of disadvantaged students would indicate that they obviously require more intervention tactics to get their writing going even in sporadic trial sessions.

Over the past several years that I have taught writing in introductory literature and applied literary criticism as well as in freshman composition classes, I have come across such isolated students who have very good writing skills and who therefore seem to respond more favorably to the kind of method described by Straub as one in which the teacher keeps in check the urge to dole out knowledge in an unfettered fashion. They do so, in part, because they know to constantly act out the belief that the best way to achieve perfection in writing is to engage in constant practice, since good writing is not primarily indicated by others but created by what is within an author. These are student writers who just need a little help to get writing that is already very good to the finish line. They need as much latitude as possible to make the most of writing because it would not seem a surprising point for them to be told that writing is a self-reflective exercise propelled far more by individual ingenuity than external control of another person who is more likely going to be an authority figure.

On the other hand, in the majority of writing classes that I have taught, a detached teacher may have absolutely no chance of making any shred of positive impact on the students' writing at all. Here I am referring to students who may be intellectually shut down and who may therefore have no sense of purpose. Not only might such students exhibit the worst form of writing imaginable, they may be found lacking even in the crucial area of self-motivation. To paraphrase, they may be bereft of the urge to try out on their own as well.

In attempting to seek ways to improve more than the teacher's fair share of some of the weak writing that may come from these kinds of student writers, the idea that I propose as a solution in this context is to return to the basics, to the old practice in which the teacher is the provider of knowledge to an actively involved class of students. This is the idea upon which American education was originally founded as an extension of British education.[1] Along the way, with liberty in progress, America increasingly saw this instructional model as a burden of Britain, shook it away, and thus threw out the baby with the bath water. This rejection of British influence has hurt American education; a redemptive return to the old practice (which might appear to the present age as a radically new way to respond to student papers), might show that approaches which have proven valuable in the past may be just what we need at this time to inject a measure of the discipline that is currently lacking in many a writing classroom in the United States.

In any evaluation (be it blind publication peer review or promotion and tenure review), we are asked to be forthright as scholar-teachers; evaluation of student papers should not be any different. An unrestrained injunction to give student writers unregulated room to negotiate creative endeavor may actually defeat a concerned teacher's efforts to be what he or she desires to be: an enabler —one who guides, pushes, assists, and encourages inexperienced student writers to produce good writing through fair and open-minded criticisms.

Many students have only a modicum of compositional skills and drive. Whether it be insisting on more intellectual depth or grammatical accuracy and rigor, the teacher can best enable, encourage, and nurture creative and critical expression among this cadre of student writers by setting a challenge and leading by inspiring example. The teacher must pay careful attention to the mechanics of writing. In addition to demanding felicity of expression and grace of utterance, which themselves provide only an appealing tone to rivet the audience or readership, good writing calls for other qualities.

As with style of presentation, mediation of the thought processes of the novice writer is needed to give his or her writing direction, to move it on course. When dealing with writing that does not hang together properly, the teacher must do more than merely place emphasis on the larger picture if the writing is to gain cohesion. Without providing detailed descriptions that connect logically, the writer cannot help the reader to form a clear picture of the subject under discussion. For the teacher to ignore local matters of detail in such writing is for him or her not to take it seriously. If the teacher is to effectively play the expected supervisory role, then, creative leverage is precisely what the novice writer needs.

In a setting where student writers require drastic motivational tactics, the ideal instructor must play a role similar, in conception and bearing, to that encapsulated in the metaphor of the concerned mentor: one who, in the words of Irene C. Goldman-Price and Melissa McFarland Pennell, serves as "a canonized saint, or perhaps author—someone whose life has been exemplary, whose worth and loyalty to the divine have been proven under duress, someone who now sits far above, offering inspiration but also, perhaps, an unreachable goal" (2).

Goldman-Price and Pennell go on to add in the same passage that the model mentor is a dependable source of knowledge: "the heel stone, pointing to the rising sun just one day of the year, in that mysterious, mythical circle whose meaning, if we could unlock it, would explain the relation between earth and sky, between humans and the universe we inhabit, between inchoate inspiration and the words necessary to commit one's imagined world to paper" (2).

For our supreme image of the ultimate mentor, all roads must, of course, justi-fiably, lead to literature, to Homer's depiction of Athene, the goddess of wis-dom, who brings Odysseus' son Telemachus into his manhood in the *Odyssey* and thus enables the young man to hold fort expeditiously, stopping all at-tempts by outsiders to violate his father's household during his exile.

Though power struggles seem not to permit some American students to learn as much as they might from foreign instructors, when teacher commen-tary is delivered with humility and tenderness, rather than in the voice of arro-gance, the challenge of being an outsider, of being someone who comes from another country and has had the experience of a different kind of life from the one American students know, can be turned into an incredible instructional opportunity. The most important thing is to make students know that distance has the special proclivity to sharpen perspective. Look at history and literature, where, time and again it is demonstrated that the best effort at helping others to bring out the best in themselves have come from total strangers.

Keen interest in how to get a sense of the best way to assist student writers in bringing the best writing out of them can trigger positive reactions in those in whose work it is shown. Every challenging moment is a magnificent one, which presents an immigrant instructor with a unique opportunity to demon-strate to the contrary: that his or her situation is more of a boom than a bane. Like the instructors who are citizens, the immigrant teacher cannot overlook the danger that every ill-prepared student who leaves college with a substan-dard degree reflects the failure of instruction. Whenever the instructor seeks to enable the wisdom of one educational system (British education in my case) to speak lovingly to another society the question of standards is not far behind.

An instructor of foreign origin can capitalize on the unlimited opportuni-ties open to him or her, and one of the first things that he or she can do is to tell classes how lucky they are to be among those living in the only place on the face of the Earth where any person of average intelligence, making minimum ef-fort, can make it to the very top of any field. In the American classroom this no-tion of crowning achievement and glory translates, in concrete terms, into the A's that figure so prominently in the spate of grades offered by professors de-spite their knowing that grade inflation harms higher education and should be brought under control, if not eliminated entirely.

By contrast, one can offer the experience of British education where a belief has been so thoroughly entrenched among lecturers that students of A-quality performance can come along only once in a great while, to the extent that one can graduate from a top British university without meeting or hearing about such a student—let alone receiving an A oneself. Although it might be tempt-ing (to judge from the proliferation of A's in American schools) to conclude that geniuses are ubiquitous in this part of the world, that we do not have documented evidence that Americans do better in the world outside the campus than the Chinese, the Japanese, and Europeans is proof of the fact that the American dream was designed to be achieveable.

On the other hand, the academically challenged students' persistent resistance to new ideas is one of the main reasons many people will hesitate to assent to the claim that America defines excellence. America has allowed too many to be left behind by the whirlwind of ascent to knowledge. What are the factors that precipitate such students' instincts, making them less receptive than other groups to new ideas? Experience shows that they tend to cling to what they believe they already know, and their attitude impedes all efforts, rendering all of the well-meaning teacher's ambitions and high expectations for the class especially inconsequential.

Many academically deficient students act in ways that suggest they have subscribed to the notion that their socio-economic situations are already predetermined, their lower performance, the natural order of things. The significance of such a mind-set lies in showing the degree to which oppositional behavior can hinder educational aspirations. The best the instructor can do is to give special encouragement to this group of students, to discourage them from the easy temptation to succumb to the belief that a different standard is expected of them because they come from roots that are historically disadvantaged. The teacher could best achieve such a goal by making one assumption unmistakably clear: Good writing abilities can serve as one of the most effective and assured gateways to socio-economic uplift.

The facts relating intellectual performance to skin color in the United States are bitter in the extreme. However, in his book *Losing the Race: Self-Sabotage in Black America*, John H. McWhorter presents overwhelming documentation of these situations, urging that society not close its eyes and pretend that the problems do not exist.[2] Taking a cue from McWhorter, the instructor can press that minority students face the situation head-on: Only effort can lead to improved performance. Let the class know that rigorous commentary holds the key to the needed remedial action because either these students are moved to clear, uncluttered, standard writing or they will be left abandoned to a gloomy future. There is no means of wresting good writing except by conversion, a complete reversal of mental attitude.

Knowing that the reproaches a committed teacher makes of student writers' mistakes will be more than compensated for by the power and sparkle enkindled by good writing, the instructor cannot afford to leave the students with an impression that the suggestions offered to improve their writing are optional. Without the strict enforcement of codes governing good writing, student writers are denied formal instruction about effective writing. Moreover, when doubt permeates a teacher's comments, students do not feel obligated to revise, and the majority give in to the temptation to take the easy way out. It is to forestall such an event that I suggest the instructor not hesitate to write unambiguous comments: while the instructor cannot guarantee that every student will take every piece of advice given, he or she can ensure that all know that it's in their best interest to not disregard corrections. For the instructor to operate a watered-down grading system is to give approval to laxity.

Of course, finding a student motivated by a real passion for writing (or genuine interest in literary theory or learning for its own sake) is every teacher's dream. So it was, when such a student was drawn to several of my own classes over the past few years. A very dynamic individual, this particular student demonstrated in the three classes he took with me (Freshman Composition, Introduction to World Literature, and then Applied Literary Criticism) that he believed strongly in students following up on all the reading and writing assignments given by the instructor. But I never got the sense that grades overshadowed his thinking. Nor did he give me any sense that I was special or doing anything extraordinary in my teaching. All I knew was that he had a deep respect for himself, and it showed through the great sense of responsibility with which he did his work. When I requested a letter of reference, from him, I was most pleasantly surprised at the graciousness and generosity he showed in the very supportive letter he wrote for me.

Even though he did not define precisely what constitutes the erudition that he found attractive in my style of instruction, I'm sure that had he been pressed he would quite easily have done so. This student's presence in my classes was a singular piece of good fortune because America is a uniquely chronic land of extreme inequalities in talent and opportunities, and I recognized that the presence of a student of his caliber is not one that is likely going to be a regular feature of my classes. Indeed, my writing classes have so far remained dominated by lazy students who have been far less enterprising than most of their disadvantaged counterparts I have encountered elsewhere and who have been far more consumed about their grade than in the qualitative work that will justify that grade.[3]

Of the many surprises of my teaching experience in recent times, none has been more troubling than this: that a student who couldn't get a coherent paragraph together on his or her own during in-class writing suddenly turns in an impecably composed take-home written assignment. As the problem of student cheaters, of plagiarism, increasingly becomes a focal one, writing teachers in the United States will have to devise ways to ensure that students are the actual authors of the works they hand in and thus they are truly deserving of the grades awarded those papers. Today one can lift an essay on virtually any subject off the internet, and the problem of internet plagiarism is truly reaching epidemic proportions. There is an overabundance of information which is making theft in the super highway irresistable to student writers, who think that the material is a free-for-all, that it is all there for the taking by anyone so inclined. How can teachers monitor student computer use, and do it in such a way as to force student writers to rely on their own efforts? Ellen Laird, an instructor of English at Hudson Valley Community College, writes in a recent essay that students steal so unconscionably from the internet, in part, because they can do so in the comfort of their "homes or dorm room[s] . . . [where] questions of ethics may be coming to seem academic only" as opposed to, say, "sitting in a library, which might, like a church, prompt behavior worthy of the setting" (B5). I believe the proliferation of computers is what makes the issue of internet policing, of monitoring its use or misuse by student writers, all the more intractable.[4]

None of this will be to indicate, of course, that students who work assiduously and honestly, and who do original work, and turn their papers in on schedule, will automatically earn top grades in writing assignments. My basic premise is very simple: Until the quality of the composition achieves the desired standard, effort alone cannot be rewarded bountifully. Student writers must avoid one reccurring error: not following instructions clearly written or spoken or outlined about assignments. In my own experience, this is the most common mistake student writers make; it is also the most difficult to deal with. But the teacher has to tell the class plainly where he or she stands in this matter.

To buttress the point of this lesson, I am often compelled to use the example of Ihie Ojenya, a classmate of mine in Secondary School in Nigeria, who habitually would study so hard that he would regularly forget the times lunch and dinner were served in the cafeteria. In preparation for the end-of-session exams, Ihie would commit to memory large chunks of information from our history textbook—dates of major events such as dynastic struggles and successions and wars as well as treaties, and the names of empires and kingdoms—and he would proudly display his knowledge to the admiration of all his classmates.

Then comes the exam and, alas, as a result of either nervousness or not finding any questions that focused on the particular parts of the huge chunks of the syllabus he had memorized, Ihie would set up his own questions and then begin to address them with the information he had gathered from his reading.

Ihie would write lengthy answers, often needing extra paper to complete the exam. Indeed Ihie would routinely end up the last person in our classes to leave the examination halls. Sadly, in the end, all that hard labor would come to nothing because our teachers said that Ihie had written all of the exams off-point, never having addressed the required questions. Having not answered any of the required questions, Ihie received an F in all his classes although our teachers conceded that the material Ihie did present was accurate and did justice to his chosen topics of discussion. Ihie dropped out of school eventually.

Here is a lesson that I draw with Ihie's expreience for the students in my writing classes: It doesn't matter how brilliant your answer may be, if it doesn't address the topic at hand, it cannot fetch you a passing grade. Consequently, one of my occupations is to clearly admonish students to follow instructions. For example, in the question, "How would you state the central theme of this poem [name mentioned] in one sentence?" the key focus is on *theme* and the limitation of *one sentence* imposed, within which the answer is to be expressed.

Thus, in responding to papers addressing such questions, I will tell students who brought out the controlling insight of the poem accurately, but who have used more than a sentence to do so, that they have certainly shown a good sense of the unifying idea of the piece but have answered the question wrongly. I let students know that not to answer the question is to engage in purposeless writing. Just as when a baby learning to walk stumbles, a good care-giver doesn't kick the baby and then say "get up," but encourages the child to try one more time, the purpose of such criticism is not to knock down the students but to teach the virtue of patience and to admonish them to take one step at a time as they try to find where they are going.

Students may fail to answer the question for a variety of reasons. They can do so because of lateness or poor class attendance or even excessive absenteeism. A student who receives an assignment from someone other than the instructor, say from a classmate, can be given the wrong wording of the assignment. Students not attending classes regularly need to be made aware that they are not following what's being done in class because they are skipping school. The teacher can deal with truancy by commenting on the guilty student's paper, "Had you been attending regularly as you should, you'd know what we've covered in this class"; this can serve as a wake-up call to the student. When students set out to not answer the question, it is a different matter: veiled resistance to the authority of the teacher.

Teacher commentary cannot be restricted to the all too evident writing problems but should radiate to cover latent behavior problems that give rise to the writing difficulties in the first place. School is increasingly becoming a place where students learn acts of defiance—concealed or overt—which they in turn inflict on the constituted authorities and their school mates. My comments are predicated upon my belief that student writers need to know that teachers pay attention to such antisocial antics as students allowing their wireless phones and beepers to ring out loudly and causing other forms of distractive behavior during class. These and other practiced forms of intimidation are unhelpful: The only way to receive competitive grades is through good writing.

Approaching writing as a totalizing experience that has the power to pull the practitioner into the deepest recesses of his or her imaginative and critical faculties, I seek to immerse my students into writing with the assumption that they need tools in order to be able to negotiate their way successfully through that strange terrain that often begins with a blank page and then subsequently stretches out as the writer aspires to his or her goal: to mass the chaos of experience into an ordered pattern.

Whether they are made as overt demands for clarification or as corrections, exploratory marginal notations, pointed end discussions, elaborations of ideas hinted at but left insufficiently developed by the student, or as copious lead queries and mental cues, my responses to student writing all have one aim: to instruct and coach the student in how to perform one particular form of writing. This procedure resembles that of an apprentice tailor being made to absorb, through constant example and exposure, practical experience and guidelines provided by the master tailor to the method of clothes design, patterning, and sewing. Detailed instruction and keen observation are critical to this process whose goal is to enable the student, by taking one step at a time, to become familiar with the general guidelines of clothes fashioning. Dissatisfaction with one's compositional performance is a requisite attitude that is needed to initiate efforts geared toward self-improvement.

Though graduate-level work presents occasion for the instructor's voice to become an even more extensive presence in student writing, sometimes the obstacles to this sort of activity may come from quite unexpected quarters. I will establish the circumstances of initial opposition I once came up against from my department chair when I gave a graduate student, who was writing his master's thesis with a committee that I sat in as a second reader, a long reading list. My department chair, who was the first reader on the committee, asked the student to disregard the reading list and restrict his research, instead, to his recollections of his oral conversations with his father about the subject matter of his investigation.

We may reasonably assume that, since my persistence that the student write a first-rate thesis, which I followed up with detailed comments that worked through the body of his writing from intellectual issues to matters of style and linguistic activities, paid off in the end (as the student successfully defended his thesis), my comments could serve as a useful model for thesis and dissertation supervision in oral literature as well as on other forms of academic writing more generally. This is how I approached his work:

Dear Moses,

I was glad for the opportunity of reading the material you gave me. This work looks highly promising. You write with considerable skill. With several revisions, you'll produce work that all of us can be very proud of. I have taken the liberty to pencil in comments on the drafts [referring to corrections of grammatical errors, non sequiturs, etc.]—hope you don't mind that. In addition, I have the following observations:

1. I would suggest that you put away your introductory chapter for now. Though it comes first in the thesis, you should write it last (after the main line of your argument has emerged fully). However, please note that, when you're ready to draft it, the aims of your research should be clearly spelled out. I see that your intention is to cover a number of issues including,

a. The identity of the toast

b. Who performs it

c. The audience of the toast, why it patronizes it

d. How the toast is learned (and may be transmitted?)

Let us have a well-developed essay on each one of these issues.

2. You have tended to have over-relied on Bruce Jackson and other critics. Of course it is always useful (even mandatory in graduate-level work) to show evidence of awareness of secondary literature, but keep in mind that, in the end, it is your own perspective that will be most important. In order for you to really show your command of the subject, you'll have to de-emphasize the secondary material. Let us have the following:

a. An idea of the number of songs/poems you are interested in. Do you have the whole corpus—including the different versions? Let us be clear about this.

b. Begin to respond to them in detail.

c. Build an argument and bring in quoted/paraphrased material only when such material is needed to support your case. We need to see your argument being developed more fully than is currently the case. What salient issues do the songs raise? Are there any areas where you differ from previous critics in your interpretation? What is your [original] contribution? What about the toasts have others ignored that you consider of importance? We need a focused and developed essay.

In fine, I believe this work is very important; with several revisions, it will certainly bring a wealth of knowledge to the subject. But this requires hard work. So, do not relent your efforts. You're on to something important. If you haven't yet seen Eric Lott's book *Love and Theft: Blackface Minstrelsy and the American Working Class* (New York: Oxford UP, 1994) and John Robert's *From Trickster to Badman: The Black Folk Hero in Slavery and Freedom* (Philadelphia: University of Pennsylvania P, 1989), please make time to see them. Even if the contents are not directly relevant, you could emulate the authors' style.

Good luck and God bless. If there's anything not clear to you about my general comments as well as those penciled into the drafts, please let me know and we can arrange a conference. My summer contact address and phone number are as given below [information supplied].

Sincerely,

Ode

In my comments, I show that I care, and I want to be a part of this particular student writer's intellectual experience. So, I make sure that I convey my desire to work with him, and I reassure him that his topic provokes an appetite for me to see more of it as its development sought to unfold in its various future drafts. What was needed next was something that the student writer should not be made to harbor any illusions about: Writing is tough; it is mental stamina, about composure, and it requires discipline and hard work. In particular, to be of any consequence, academic writing must spring from a labor of love, in which confusion has no place and in which planning is critical so that a thesis can be firmly established and explored in an orderly manner before a conclusion is reached. As such, clarity of focus, coherence, and logic are essential components of this activity. Therefore, no detail was too small for my attention. I marked up and corrected every line the student had written, polishing up his prose, and restoring the argument, where it got lost in a muddle of quotations and plot summaries.

To prevent this student writer from being misled into engaging in the purposeless act of attempting to reinvent the wheel all over again, I introduced him to the established ground rules for scholarly research and writing by stressing the importance of examining previous commentaries on his primary sources. To paraphrase, I encouraged him to join the conversation with the critics who preceded him. In inviting him to join the disciplinary community of writers of research papers, only by being keenly aware of tradition, I urge, can this student writer's genuinely fresh contributions converge. To get past the roadblocks that keep student writers from accepting corrections, I praised him for what he had done well, and I urged him to listen and support me in my effort to translate his intentions into polished writing. The technique worked so perfectly because Moses listened and produced a remarkably closely argued thesis, free of cant and impeccably designed and executed.

But what about those pieces of student writing in which sole supervisory responsibility does not lie with an instructor? What about cases in which the instructor is a second reader? Should the instructor still give it his or her all? The answer is, of course, yes. Instructors must remain equally concerned as much with style as with content as well. I recall, for example, when the drafts of Alice's master's thesis were being sent around, and I made up my mind that I was going to send them back with more than the usual kind remarks even though I was sitting on her committee as a distant third reader. Presented below are the notes that I took to my first conference with her on April 5, 1999:

As you prepare your thesis, please be aware that all *significant* research is about a lack; about omissions or gaps, in the existing body of scholarship that would need to be made up for, filled. Since others have written about your subject [Harriet Beecher Stowe], what is missing in their interpretations that you would like to redress, make up for? Consider the following:

1. Draw up a typology to guide you in your review of the existing literature. In other words, group the existing literary responses to Stowe's work. Avoid simple itemization.

2. Point out the critics' main points as well as the deficiences in their arguments in relation to your topic. Tell us how your work differs in emphasis. What is the intended contribution of your reading? What are you bringing to Stowe scholarship?

3. It usually wouldn't be enough to simply allude to the critics in an ad-hoc fashion; systematic, detailed review is essential.

4. After all these years of writing being done on Stowe, why are you taking her on at this time? A detailed topic justification is mandatory.

5. The references I sent to you through Dr. [her first reader] are very good; let me encourage you again to use all the eight titles [no longer have a record of these!]

Going over the draft of this student writer's thesis, I could see right away that there were substantive problems that needed to be addressed, and I raised these issues in discussion with the student—the writer had simply meandered through a hodge-podge of Stowe criticism without providing a running thread through them. An overarching argument was missing; without having justified her rather lean selection from what is evidently a very extensive body of criticism being plied through, the discussion wasn't as convincing as the writer desired.

Alice's thesis was crying out for a sense of focus. Because of Alice's refusal (or inability) to make use of cross-references, her utilization of the existing scholarship still left much to be desired. My commentary primarily sought to take care of these problems. Alas, this was the last draft of Alice's thesis that I saw; Alice came up for the thesis defense, and I received the final draft: She still hadn't incorporated any of the changes I had recommended, and only two or three of the books that I had suggested were listed in the lean bibliography, though there was no evidence by way of either citation or summarizing and paraphrasing that she actually had consulted any one of them.

Alice received the master's degree. I thought I had worked magnificiently to help Alice, a graduate student, improve the thesis writing assignment. But the student chose to be unreceptive and still was rewarded with a degree.

This brings me to the final category of student resistance: the letter that Mark, a student wrote to express his frustration about his perception that I was making my Spring 1997 English Composition class too demanding for his comfort. Eloquently making the case for less rigor in my handling of the class, he wrote as follows:

Dear Dr. Ogede:
Rather than have a conference with you, I am writing this letter to you. As you know I had Composition I under your instruction, and I did not complain during that time. However, this semester (second semester) taking Composition II is becoming frustrating and stressful.

At the beginning of second semester (1996–1997), you stated to the class that you were going to follow the class syllabus. However, your continuing to assign additional readings that are not on the syllabus is getting on my last nerves and it is stressful. It is enough to keep up with the syllabus, plus the other classes that I have to do academic work for. Therefore, the additional books that you are assigning to read are taking too much time from my other responsibilities.

I would greatly appreciate it if you would follow the class syllabus.

Sincerely,

Mark

Scenes of outrage like this starkly reveal the grave oppositions writing teachers face daily in the classroom. Nothing that Mark is saying will be new to those who have taught any of those courses, like writing, that cannot be taught in a predictable manner. The course started out easy and became increasingly difficult as we tried to transit from elementary material. As the going got tougher, students like Mark began to complain about being "stressed out."

Laurie A. Finke has eminently remarked about a similar context: "To be sure, not every student becomes depressed, but many do, enough to affect negatively the dynamics of the classroom" (154). To this, I want to add only that the rippling effects of a single disgruntled student's distractive behavior can be particularly devastating in a large undergraduate classroom such as Mark's freshman composition class. He wanted the class instruction to be conducted within certain confines, within the boundaries of limited sensibilities; he wanted to narrow the range of his own intellectual adventures. By turns admonitory, conciliatory, or both, he focuses as much on what are his expectations of the class as on the betrayal, the breach of faith that he believes the teacher's challenging handling of them represents. I refused to bow to his wishes; consequently he began to defy assignment orders and to dispute the comments that I wrote on his papers. When I asked for clarification, he said his point was clear enough. He objected to my correcting his grammar and other writing problems. Finally, Mark brought his mother who, like her son, asserted that I needed to relax the pressure of work being put on the class. Professional integrity meant that I had to persuade both mother and son that chafing about the course's difficulty was going to be ultimately harmful. He subsequently tried to put up with the requirements of the class by doing his best and he received the eventual grade of a B. When those with less talent resort to other kinds of tactics, such as writing letters to say to me that they are on probation or would jeopardize a certain scholarship if they do receive less than a certain specified grade in my class, they are equally unsuccessful. I try to let everyone know that I cannot honor any requests to negotiate grades, which must be earned by diligence, hard work, and demonstrable performance.[5]

My emphasis on both the nitty gritty and the larger issues in the design and structure of student papers places my style in opposition to that of the more liberal instructor described by Richard Straub in his essay "The Concept of Control in Teacher Response." I believe that if student writers can be open to feedback, they have a lot to learn from enthusiastic teachers to help them take their writing competencies to another level. If they decide not to, they have to face up to the final consequences: The grade is the only weapon that teachers have to wield; sometimes they can use it, but there are bound to be occasions when they won't. To try to help students improve their writing, and do it with every rigor, is what writing teachers should continue doing, as their professional role demands. However, it goes with the territory for students to refuse help. It is also part of the job for teachers to reward students, when they can, with grades that reflect performance. I believe that, if a teacher can help just one student at a time in his or her class not to give up on creativity, it is worth the effort.

NOTES

1. While Noel Annan provides a telling chronicle in his recent book, *The Dons: Mentors, Eccentrics and Geniuses* (1999), of the practices that make intellectual life in two of Britain's most prestigious universities—Cambridge and Oxford—models of academic culture, in *Literature: An Embattled Profession*, Carl Woodring refers to the British roots of early American education, offering a witty account of the history of American students' resistance to the "regimented progression, tests, and ranking" that Americans increasingly came to associate with British education (61). See also William H. Pritchard's *The English Papers: A Teaching Life* for details regarding the way values such as passion animated teaching in the past in America, as well as Jacques Barzun's *Begin Here: The Forgotten Conditions of Teaching and Learning* for the dangers posed by the decline of those kinds of cultures in contemporary times.

2. Though McWhorter's account of the poor school performance of young African Americans from comfortable middle-class backgrounds relative to their white peers has drawn some criticism, I believe the parameters of his study can be usefully applied to the educational achievement of young African American school children from other backgrounds as well. McWhorter, a linguistics professor, is an African American, and arguments are based on history and statistics as well as his own first-hand experiences of the crises he explores.

3. I refer to the fact that in schools across America students need to be motivated, whereas students in many other countries seem to know the importance of learning for its own sake. As everyone knows, America has more writing programs than any other country in the world. But although the shelves of libraries of colleges and universities across the country are filled with textbooks and scholarly titles on composition targeted at the student population, it does seem as if these books are conveniently ignored by many students who have other priorities.

4. The problem of internet plagiarism should not be considered in isolation of the rising incidents of other types of internet fraud, such as people putting false notices on the web as a hoax to raise interest in a particular product in the stock market, for example. But while changing students' attitudes could not be realized without a more profound cultural transformation involving a redefinition of ownership, the increasing attention being devoted by teachers in America to the issue of student theft of ideas holds out great promise for its control if not for its total elimination, and teachers' success in this endeavor will in no small measure be dependent on the inflexible stand they can take against the phenomenon of academic dishonesty as a whole as well as on their will to apply stringent measures geared toward punishing student offenders when caught in the act of internet plagiarism in particular.

5. Letters like these are frequent in my classes, and they mirror the excessive preoccupation with grades in America. Whenever I receive one, I immediately have a conference with the author to make clear my strong objection to negotiating grades with students.

WORKS CITED

Annan, Noel. *The Dons: Mentors, Eccentrics and Geniuses.* Chicago: University of Chicago Press, 1999.

Barzun, Jacques. *Begin Here: The Forgotten Conditions of Teaching and Learning.* Chicago: University of Chicago Press, 1991.

Burnham, Michelle. *Captivity and Sentiment.* Hanover and London: University of New England Press, 1997.

Finke, Laurie A. "Pedagogy of the Depressed: Feminism, Poststructuralism, and Pedagogical Practice." In *Teaching Contemporary Theory to Undergraduates,* edited by Dianne F. Sadoff, and William Cain, 154–68. New York: Modern Language Association of America, 1994.

Goldman-Price, Irene C., and Melissa McFarland Pennell, eds. *American Literary Mentors.* Gainesville: University Press of Florida, 1999.

Laird, Ellen. "Internet Plagiarism: We All Pay the Price." *The Chronicle of Higher Education Review,* July 13, 2001, B5.

McWhorter, John H. *Losing the Race: Self-Sabotage in Black America.* New York: The Free Press, 2000.

Pritchard, William H. *English Papers: A Teaching Life.* Saint Paul, MN: Gray Wolf Press, 1995.

Straub, Richard. "The Concept of Control in Teacher Response: Defining the Varieties of 'Directive' and 'Facilitative' Commentary." *College Composition and Communication* 47 (May 1996): 223–51.

———. *A Sourcebook for Responding to Student Writing.* Cresskill, NJ: Hampton Press, 1999.

Woodring. Carl. *Literature: An Embattled Profession.* New York: Columbia University Press, 1999.

SUGGESTED READINGS

Delbanco, Andrew. *Required Reading*. New York: Farrar, Straus and Giroux, 1997.

Hartman, Saidiya. *Scenes of Subjection*. New York: Oxford University Press, 1995.

Kazin, Alfred. *God and the American Writer*. New York: Knopf, 1997.

Lott, Eric. *Love and Theft: Blackface Minstrels and the American Working Class*. New York: Oxford University Press, 1994.

Roberts, John. *From Trickster to Badman: The Black Folk Hero in Slavery and Freedom*. Philadelphia: University of Pennsylvannia Press, 1989.

Simons, Thomas. *Erotic Reckonings: Mastery and Apprenticeship in the Work of Poets and Lovers*. Urbana and Chicago: University of Illinios Press, 1994.

Sollors, Werner. *Neither Black nor White*. New York: Oxford University Press, 1996.

Sundqvist, Eric. *To Wake the Nations*. Cambridge: Belknap, Harvard University Press, 1993.

Selected Bibliography

Ahern, Susan W. "Conducting a Successful Local Job Search." *Ade Bulletin* 129 (Fall 2001): 21–23.

Annan, Noel. *The Dons: Mentors, Eccentrics and Geniuses*. Chicago: University of Chicago Press, 1999.

Anson, Chris M. "Distant Voices: Teaching and Writing in a Culture of Technology." *College English* 61.3 (1999): 261–80.

———. "Reflective Reading: Developing Thoughtful Ways to Respond to Students' Writing." In *Evaluating Writing*, edited by Charles R. Cooper and Lee Odel. Urbana, IL: NCTE, 1999.

Babad, E. "The 'Teacher's Pet' Phenomenon, Students' Perceptions of Teachers' Differential Behavior, and Students' Morale." *Journal of Education Psychology* 87 (1995): 361–74.

Baker, J. "Teacher-Student Interaction in Urban At-Risk Classrooms: Differential Behavior, Relationship Quality, and Student Satisfaction with School." *The Elementary School Journal* 100 (1999): 57.

Bakhtin, Mikhail M. "Epic and Novel: Toward a Methodology for the Study of the Novel." In *The Dialogic Imagination: Four Essays*, translated by Caryl Emerson and Michael Holquist, 3–40. Austin: University of Texas Press, 1981.

Barzun, Jacques. *Begin Here: The Forgotten Conditions of Teaching and Learning*. Chicago: University of Chicago Press, 1991.

Beach, R. "Self-Evaluation Strategies of Extensive Revisers and Non-Revisers." *College Composition and Communication* 27.2 (1976): 160–64.

Beach, R., and L.S. Bridwell, eds. *New Directions in Composition Research.* New York: Guilford Press, 1984.

Bereiter, C., and M. Scardemalia. "Levels of Inquiry in Writing Research." In *Research on Writing: Principles and Methods*, edited by P. Mosenthal, L. Tamor, and S.A. Walmsley, 3–25. New York: Longman, 1984.

Bernard, W.H., and W.C. Huckins. *Humanism in the Classroom: An Eclectic Approach to Teaching and Learning.* Boston: Allyn and Bacon, 1974.

Bishop, Wendy. *Released into Language: Options for Teaching Creative Writing.* 2nd ed. Portland, ME: Calendar Islands, 1998.

———. "Responding to Creative Writing: Students as Teachers and the Executive Summary." In *Teaching Writing Creatively*, edited by David Starkey, 180–86. Portsmouth, NH: Heinemann, Boynton, Cook, 1998.

Bishop, Wendy, and Hans Ostrum, eds. *Colors of a Different Horse: Rethinking Creative Writing Theory and Pedagogy.* Urbana, IL: NCTE, 1994.

Bizarro, Patrick. "Reading the Creative Writing Course: The Teacher's Many Selves." In *Colors of a Different Horse: Rethinking Creative Writing Theory and Pedagogy*, edited by Wendy Bishop and Hans Ostrum, 234–47. Urbana, IL: NCTE, 1994.

Brannon, Lil, and C.H. Knoblauch. "On Students' Rights to Their Own Texts: A Model of Teacher Response." *College Composition and Communication* 33 (1982): 157–66.

Brophy, J.E. "Conceptualizing Student Motivation." *Educational Psychologist* 18 (1983): 200–15.

Bruffee, Kenneth A. "Peer Tutoring and 'The Conversation of Mankind.'" In *The Harcourt Brace Guide to Peer Tutoring*, edited by Toni-Less Capossela. New York: Harcourt Brace, 1998.

Burkland, J., and N. Grimm. "Motivating through Responding." *Journal of Teaching Writing* 5 (1986): 237–47.

Burnham, Michelle. *Captivity and Sentiment.* Hanover and London: University of New England Press, 1997.

Capossela, Toni-Less, ed. *The Harcourt Brace Guide to Peer Tutoring.* New York: Harcourt Brace, 1998.

Connors, Robert J., and Andrea Lunsford. "Teachers' Rhetorical Comments on Student Papers." *College Composition and Communication* 44 (1993): 200–23.

Cooper, Charles R., and Lee Odel, eds. *Evaluating Writing.* Urbana, Illinois: NCTE, 1999.

Elbow, Peter. *Embracing Contraries: Explorations in Learning and Teaching.* New York: Oxford University Press, 1986.

———. "Ranking, Evaluating, and Liking: Sorting Out Three Forms of Judgment." *College English* (February 1993): 187–206.

Engelberg, R.A. "Student Perspective on Grades." Ph.D. diss., University of Washington, 1988.

Feynman, Richard P., Robert B. Leighton, and Matthew Sands. *The Feyman Lectures on Physics, Volumes I–III.* Reading, MA: Addison-Wesley, 1963.

Finke, Laurie A. "Pedagogy of the Depressed: Feminism, Poststructuralism, and Pedagogical Practice." In *Teaching Contemporary Theory to Undergraduates,* edited by Dianne F. Sadoff and William Cain, 154–68. New York: Modern Language Association of America, 1994.

Freire, P. *Pedagogy of Hope.* New York: Continuum Publishing, 1994.

Frymier, A.B. and M.L. Houser. "The Teacher-Student Relationship as an Interpersonal Relationship." *Communication Education* 49 (2000): 207–19.

Fusani, D.S. "Extra-Class Communication: Frequency, Immediacy, Self-Disclosure, and Satisfaction in Student-Faculty Interaction Outside the Classroom." *Journal of Applied Communication Research* 22 (1994): 232.

Gay, Pamela. "Dialogizing Response in the Writing Classroom: Students Answer Back." *Journal of Basic Writing* (Spring 1998): 1–17.

Goldman-Price, Irene C. and Melissa McFarland Pennell, eds. *American Literary Mentors.* Gainesville, FL: University Press of Florida, 1999.

Graves, Richard L., ed. *The Writer on Her Work.* 2nd ed. Upper Montclair, NJ: Boynton/Cook, 1984.

Guyton, D.C. "Good Teaching: Passionate Performances." *English Journal* 84 (1995): 59–60.

Hacker, Diana. 1989. *A Writer's Reference.* 3rd ed. New York: St. Martin's Press, 1997.

Hanna, F.J., W.B. Talley, and M. H. Guindon. "The Power of Perception: Toward a Model of Cultural Oppression and Liberation." *Journal of Counseling and Development* 78 (2000): 430–41.

Hensley, Dennis E., and Holly G. Miller. *Write on Target.* Boston: The Writer, Inc., 1995.

Hillocks, George. *Research in Teaching Composition.* Urbana, IL: NCTE, 1986.

———. *Research on Written Composition: New Directions for Teaching.* Urbana, IL: NCTE, 1986.

hooks, b. *Teaching to Transgress: Education as the Practice of Freedom.* New York: Routledge, 1994.

Horner, Bruce. "Rethinking the 'Sociality' of Error: Teaching Editing as Negotiation." In *Representing the "Other": Basic Writers and the Teaching of Basic Writing,* edited by Bruce Horner and Min-Zhan Lu, 139–65. Urbana, IL: NCTE, 1999.

Kantor, K.J. "Classroom Contexts and the Development of Writing Institutions: An Ethnographic Case Study." In *New Directions in Composition Research,* edited by R. Beach and L.S. Bridwell, 72–94. New York: Guilford Press, 1984.

Keefe, C. "The Ethical Decision—Points for the Teacher in Relation to Student Perceptions of Unethical Behaviors." Paper presented at the 68th Annual Meeting of the Speech Communication Association, Louisville, Kentucky, November 4–7, 1982.

Kemp, Fred. "Writing Dialogically: Bold Lessons from Electronic Text." In *Reconceiving Writing, Rethinking Writing Instruction*, edited by Joseph Petraglia, 179–94. Mahwah, NJ: Lawrence Erlbaum Associates, 1995.

Knoblauch, C.H., and Lil Brannon. "Teacher Commentary on Student Writing: The State of the Art." *Freshman English News* 10 (Fall 1981): 1–4.

———. "Teacher Commentary on Student Writing: The State of the Art." In *The Writer on Her Work*, edited by Richard L. Graves, 285–91. 2nd ed. Upper Montclair, NJ: Boynton/Cook, 1984.

Laird, Ellen. "Internet Plagiarism: We All Pay the Price." *The Chronicle of Higher Education Review* (July 13, 2001): B5.

Lamott, Anne. *Bird by Bird: Some Instructions on Writing and Life*. New York: Anchor-Doubleday, 1994.

Lauer, J.M., and W.J. Asher. *Composition Research/Empirical Designs*. New York: Oxford University Press, 1988.

Leach, Leslie R., Nancy A. Knowles, and Tracy D. Duckart. "Living the Myth: Merging Student and Teacher Needs in Responding Effectively and Efficiently to Student Papers." Paper presented at the Annual Conference of the English Council of California Community and Two-Year Colleges, San Francisco, California, October 16–18, 1997.

Lewis, John F., and Susan C. Hastings. *Sexual Harassment in Education*. 2nd ed. Cleveland, OH: Squires, Sanders, and Dempster, 1994.

Lindemann, Erica C. *A Rhetoric for Writing Teachers*. Oxford: Oxford University Press, 1994.

"Marking Strategies." Mantex Information Design. http://mantex.co.uk/books/marks01.htm

Martin, Lee. "My Other, My Self: Participants and Spectators in 'Introductory' Fiction Writing Workshops." In *Teaching Writing Creatively*, edited by David Starkey, 172–79. Portsmouth, NH: Heinemann, Boynton, Cook, 1998.

McWhorter, John H. *Losing the Race: Self-Sabotage in Black America*. New York: The Free Press, 2000.

Miller, Susan. *Textual Carnivals: The Politics of Composition*. Carbondale: Southern Illinois University Press, 1991.

Milton, Ohmer. *On College Teaching: A Guide to Contemporary Practices*. San Francisco: Jossey-Bass Publishers, 1978.

Moffett, James, and Betty Jane Wagner. *Student-Centered Language Arts and Reading, K–13: A Handbook for Teachers*. 3rd ed. Boston: Houghton Mifflin, 1983.

Moulton, P., M. Moulton, M. Housewright, and K. Bailey. "Gifted and Talented: Exploring the Positive and Negative Aspects of Labeling." *Roeper Review* 21 (1998): 153–54.

Mutnick, Deborah. *Writing in an Alien World: Basic Writing and the Struggle for Equality in Higher Education*. Portsmouth, NH: Boynton/Cook Publishers, 1996.

Newell, George E. "The Effects of Written Between-Draft Responses on Students' Writing and Reasoning about Literature." *Written Communication* 2.3 (July 1994): 311–48.

Orange, Carolyn. *25 Biggest Mistakes Teachers Make and How to Avoid Them.* Thousand Oaks, CA: Corwin, 2000.

Ostrum, Hans. "'Carom Shots': Reconceptualizing Imitation and Its Uses in Creative Writing Courses." In *Teaching Writing Creatively*, edited by David Starkey. Portsmouth, NH: Heinemann, Boynton, Cook, 1998.

Parr, M., and L. Valerius. "Professors' Perceptions of Student Behaviors." *College Student Journal* 33 (1999): 414.

Patterson, C.H. *Humanistic Education.* Englewood Cliffs, NJ: Prentice-Hall, 1973.

Payne, Ruby K., Philip DeVol, and Terie Dreussi Smith. *Bridges Out of Poverty.* Highlands, TX: RFT Publishing, 1999.

Perlmutter, D.D. "Students Are Blithely Ignorant; Professors Are Bitter." *The Chronicle of Higher Education*, July 27, 2001, B20.

Perrine, R.M. "Please See Me: Students' Reactions to Professor's Request as a Function of Attachment and Perceived Support." *The Journal of Experimental Education* 68 (1999): 60–72.

Petraglia, Joseph, ed. *Reconceiving Writing, Rethinking Writing Instruction.* Mahwah, NJ: Lawrence Erlbaum Associates, 1995.

Pichaske, D.R. "When Students Make Sexual Advances." *The Chronicle of Higher Education*, (1995): B1–2.

Podis, Leonard A. and Joanne M. Podis. "Improving Our Responses to Student Writing: A Process-Oriented Approach." *Rhetoric Review* 5 (1986): 90–98.

Pritchard, William H. *English Papers: A Teaching Life.* Saint Paul, MN: Gray Wolf Press, 1995.

Proett, Jackie, and Kent Gill. *The Writing Process in Action: A Handbook for Teachers.* Urbana, IL: NCTE, 1986.

Purkey, W.J., and J.M. Novak. *Inviting Success: A Self-Concept Approach to Teaching and Learning.* Belmont, CA: Wadsworth Publishing, 1984.

Rickey, H.W., and M.H. Rickey. "Nonverbal Behavior in the Classroom." *Psychology in the Classroom* 15 (1978): 571–76.

Rothgery, David. "So What Do We Do Now? Necessary Directionality as the Writing Teacher's Response to Racist, Sexist, Homophobic Papers." *College Composition and Communication* 44.2 (May 1993): 241–47.

Sacks, Peter. *Generation X Goes to College: An Eye-Opening Account of Teaching in Postmodern America.* Chicago: Open House Court Press, 1996.

Sadoff, Dianne F., and William Cain, eds. *Teaching Contemporary Theory to Undergraduates.* New York: Modern Language Association of America, 1994.

Schor, Ira. *When Students Have Power: Negotiating Authority in a Critical Pedagogy.* Chicago: University of Chicago Press, 1996.

Schor, Ira, and P. Freire. *A Pedagogy for Liberation: Dialogues on Transformative Education.* New York: Bergin and Garvey, 1987.

Shaughnessy, Mina P. "Diving In: An Introduction to Basic Writing." *College Composition and Communication* 27 (1976): 234–39.

———. *Errors and Expectations: A Guide for the Teacher of Basic Writing.* New York: Oxford University Press, 1977.

Smith, Summer. "The Genre of the End Comment: Conventions in Teacher Responses to Student Writing." *College Composition and Communication* 48.2 (1997): 249–68.

Sommers, Nancy. "Responding to Student Writing." *College Composition and Communication* 33 (1982): 148–56.

Soven, Margot Iris. *Teaching Writing in Middle and Secondary Schools: Theory, Research, and Practice.* Boston: Allyn and Bacon, 1995.

Starkey, David, ed. *Teaching Writing Creatively.* Portsmouth, NH: Heinemann, Boynton, Cook, 1998.

Straub, Richard. "The Concept of Control in Teacher Response: Defining the Varieties of 'Directive' and 'Facilitative' Commentary." *College Composition and Communication* 47 May (1996): 223–51.

———. *A Sourcebook for Reponding to Student Writing.* Cresskill, NJ: Hampton Press, 1999.

———. "Students' Reactions to Teacher Comments: An Exploratory Study." *Research in the Teaching of English* 31.1 (1997): 91–119.

Straub, Richard and Ronald F. Lunsford. *Twelve Readers Reading.* Creskill, NJ: Hampton Press, 1995.

Sundqvist, Eric. *To Wake the Nations.* Cambridge: Belknap, Harvard University Press, 1993.

Tal, Z., and E. Babad. "The Teacher's Pet Phenomenon: Rate of Occurrence, Correlates, and Psychological Costs." *Journal of Educational Psychology* 82 (1990): 637–45.

———. "The 'Teacher's Pet' Phenomenon as Viewed by Israeli Teachers and Students." *The Elementary School Journal* 90 (1989): 96–108.

Tarvers, Josephine Koster. *Teaching in Progress: Theories, Practices, and Scenarios.* New York: Longman, 1998.

Van Horn, J.E., W.B. Schaufeli, and D. Enzmann. "Teacher Burnout and Lack of Reciprocity." *Journal of Applied Social Psychology* 29 (1999): 91–108.

Weinstein, C.S. "Teacher Education Students' Preconceptions of Teaching." *Journal of Teacher Education* 40 (1989): 53–60.

Wentz, Richard E. "The Merits of Professors Emeriti." *The Chronicle of Higher Education*, December 14, 2001, B5.

Wheatley, Margaret J. *Leadership and the New Science: Discovering Order in a Chaotic World.* San Francisco: Berret-Koehler, 1999.

Woodring, Carl. *Literature: An Embattled Profession.* New York: Columbia University Press, 1999.

Ziv, N. "The Effect of Teacher Comments on the Writing of Four College Freshmen." In *New Directions in Composition Research*, edited by R. Beach and L.S. Bridwell, 362–79. New York: Guilford Press, 1984

Index

academically challenged or deficient students, problem of effective teaching among the group, 107

African cities, 8

Ahern, Susan, 8–9

American education, as an extension of British education, 104

Annan, Noel, 116

apathy in American university classrooms, 2

Babad, E., 33

Baker, J., 32, 34, 37

Barzun, Jacques, 116

Begin Here (Barzun), 116

behavior problems, in students' acts of defiance, 40, 53, 110, 114–115

Bernard, W., 97

Bishop, Wendy, 82, 85, 86, 88

Bizarro, Patrick, 82, 88

black institutions of higher education v. white institutions of higher education, funding inequities and shortage of facilities hindering performance and faculty and student morale, 2, 8–9

British education, as foundation of American education, 104, 106

British-style university lecture hall v. American college student-participatory or discussion teaching mode, 1–2

Bruffee, Kenneth, 60

Burkland, Jill, 13

Camus, Albert, 54

cassette tape mode teacher commentary, 91

complimentary v. prescriptive commentary, 76

conferencing approach to teacher commentary, 90

Connors, Robert, 72

conventional product-based approach to teacher commentary, 83

copious lead queries as process in teacher commentary, 111

demands for clarification, as process in teacher commentary, 111

dialogic or dialogical approach to teacher commentary, 46, 49

The Dons (Noel Annan), 116, 117

Donne, John, 66

educational standards, the struggle to maintain high standards, 6

Elbow, Peter, 64, 70, 71, 72, 74, 75

electronic mail, as tool for teacher commentary, 68

English Composition, 65

enthusiastic teachers, decline of, 116

established ground rules for scholarly research, as part of teacher commentary, 113

exploratory marginal notations, 111

faculty politics, role in undermining academics' power and influence, 9

fair grading, necessity of, 6, 90

favoritism, its destructive effects in the classroom, 29, 31

Feynman, R. P., 58–59

Finke, Laurie, 115

formal instruction, as a critical tool of effective writing, 107

Freire, Paulo, 96, 99

Gay, Pamela, 51, 53, 54

Generation X Goes to College (Sacks), 4–5, 39–40, 45, 48

Generation X students, 45, 47

Gill, Kent, 72

Glasser, William, 61

Goldman-Price, Irene C., 105

grade inflation, as harmful to education, 40, 41

grade as teacher's weapon for student control, 116

grading, its role in instruction, 5, 83

graduate-level instruction, 95

graduate-level work, 111

graduate students, 36

Hacker, Diana, 41–42

Herbert, George, 66

high school v. university student writing standards, 53

Hillocks, George, 73

hooks, bell, 99

Honors English Composition, 65

Huckins, W., 97

Hudson Valley Community College, 109

ill-prepared students, problem of teaching, 106

immigrant teachers as assets, 3, 106

inexperienced student writers, 15

intercoder reliability, 15

internet plagiarism, 117

Introduction to the English Language, 65

Introduction to Literature, 65

instructors of foreign origin, 106

Iowa Fiction Workshops, 82

Ivy-League, as setting of worst forms of ignorance 2; and as site of sophisticated intellectual inquiry, 2

Kantor, Kenneth, 18, 20

King, Martin-Luther, Jr., 52, 53

Knoblauch, C. H., 71, 72, 82

Laird, Ellen, 109

laissez faire academic climate, 104

Lammont, Anne, 87, 88

late Victorian England v. contemporary America, 59

"Letter from Birmingham Jail" (Martin Luther King, Jr.), 52–53

limitations of the "Ideal Text" approach to teacher commentary, 83

limited sensibilities of students, 115

Lindemann, Erika, 28

Lott, Eric, 112

Lunsford, Anrea, 71, 72

The Lyceum, 59

magnetic approach to teacher commentary, 90

Mainland China, 36

marginalia, 60, 64, 68

marginal learner, 34

marginal notations, 21, 22

Martin, Lee, 87, 88

McFarland, Pennell, 105–106

McWhorter, John H., 107, 116–117

mental cues, 111

mentor-mentee relationship, as ideal condition for effective teacher commentary, 105–106

Miller, Susan, 55, 56

Moffett, James, 73, 74

motivational tactics targeted at underachieving student, 105

National Association for Educational Progress, 72

NBA (National Basketball Association) players v. academics, 9

Norwergian, 35

Novak, J., 97

Odyssey (Homer), 106

On College Teaching (Ohmer Milton), 9

Ostrum, Hans, 82, 87

Patterson, C. H., 98, 101

Pedagogy of Hope (Paulo Freire), 96

peer criticism, as tool to facilitate teacher commentary, 23

Pichaske, D. R., 37–38

plagiarism, problem of detecting and stopping the illicit practice, 108

Plato, 30

platonic dialog, as a method of teacher commentary, 30

post-Watergate experience, as a contributor to student writing problems, 45

Pritchard, William H., 116

Proet, Jackie, 72

Quality School, The (William Glasser), 61

Robert, John, 112, 118

Sacks, Peter, 4–5, 44, 45

Secondary School in Nigeria, 109

seminar mode teacher commentary, 92

Shaughnessy, Mina, 71

"The Sisyphus" (Albert Camus), 54

Skinner, B. F., 75

Smith, Summer, 59

Socrates, 59

Sommers, Nancy, 71, 83

Soven, Margot, 72

students intellectually shut down, 104

students' preoccupation with grades, 89

student-teacher relationships, 31

student truancy, 110

Straub, Richard, 12–14, 20, 44, 71, 72, 103–104, 117

student computer use, problem of monitoring, 109

supervisory responsibility, 113

teacher commentary as exploratory procedure, 7

teacher's passion, 25

teacher's pet, transformed into a positive instructional tool, 29–36

thesis writing assignment, 114

truancy, 110

United States, 5, 8
University of Toledo, 49–50

Wagner, Betty, 73, 74
Wheatley, Margaret, 58
writing as mental stamina, 113
writing as a totalizing experience, 110

Writer's Reference, A (Diana Hacker),
    41–42
Writing Program at the University of
    California at Santa Barbara (UCSB),
    11–13

Yeats, W. B., 64–65

Ziv, Nina 17–18, 20

About the Editor and Contributors

BONNIE BEEDLES, who received her M.A. in English from the University of California, Santa Barbara, taught for several years in UCSB's Writing Program. Her recent publications include the college composition textbooks *Academic Communities/Disciplinary Conventions*, with Michael Petracca (2001) and *A Sequence for Academic Writing*, with Laurence Behrens and Leonard J. Rosen (2001). She has ongoing interests in education and technology, popular culture, media literacy, and rhetoric in the social sciences. She is currently working on several writing projects.

MARILYN D. BUTTON is professor of English at Lincoln University in Lincoln, Pennsylvania. Currently on leave teaching at Taylor University in Upland, Indiana, she has co-edited (with Toni Reed) *The Foreign Woman in British Literature: Exotics, Aliens, and Outsiders* (1999). Her published articles and conference presentations have focused on women writers, including Flannery O'Connor, Muriel Spark, and nineteenth-century feminist Frances Milton Trollope. She has ongoing interests in the international dimension of English literature.

MARGARET CHRISTIAN is associate professor of English at Pennsylvannia State University Berks-Lehigh Valley College, where she teaches courses in sixteenth-century English literature and composition. The recipient of fellowships from the National Endowment for the Humanities (1992 and 1999), her articles on sixteenth-century English literature and religious discourse have appeared in *Spencer Studies, Sixteenth Century Journal,* and *Christianity and Literature.* She has previously taught composition at the University of California, Los Angeles; at Union College in Lincoln, Nebraska; at the Beijing Languages Institute in Beijing, China; and at Kutztown University in Kutztown, Pennsylvannia.

MARY THERESA HALL is associate professor of English at Thiel College, Greenville, Pennsylvania. She received her M.A. in Literature from Carnegie Mellon University and her Ph.D. in English from Duquesne University. She has completed her first book, *Country Parsons, Country Poets: George Herbert and Gerard Manley Hopkins as Spiritual Autobiographers* (1993). Her publications and areas of research interest are linguistics, the history of the English language, Medieval literature, Renaissance literature, world literature, spiritual autobiography, secondary and higher education, and pragmatic linguistics. Among her most recent publications are an essay on the contributions of St. Therese of Lisieux in *Catholic Women Writers: A Bio-Bibliographical Sourcebook* and an essay in a forthcoming book honoring Peter Elbow.

LOUISE MAYNOR serves as associate professor in the department of English at North Carolina Central University in Durham, North Carolina. Professor Maynor received her M.A in English from Appalachian State University and her doctoral degree in English Education from Duke University and has taught at Carson-Newman College and The University of Georgia. With L. Norflett, R. Lawson, and G.L. Yearwood, Professor Maynor has co-edited the NCCU-sponsored Arts and Humanities course guide, *The Impact of the New South on the Arts and Humanities in America: 1896 to the Present* (1997).

THOMAS EARL MIDGETTE, an associate professor, is the director of the Institute for the Study of Minority Issues at North Carolina Central University. He has previously held appointments at Duke University, the University of Pennsylvania, The Anti-Defamation League, The University of Arkansas, University of Akron, and Michigan State University. He is the author of several articles and reviews in such journals as *The Journal of Cross-Cultural Psychology, Journal of Multicultural Counseling and Development, The Scholar's Edge,* and *The Third World International Journal and Review.*

ODE OGEDE was educated at Ahmadu Bello University, in Zaria, Nigeria, where he did a Ph.D. on African literature. He is currently professor of English at North Carolina Central University, where he teaches African literature, folklore, literary theory, American literature, and multicultural literature. He has published books on Chinua Achebe, Ayi Kwei Armah, and folklore. His books include *Art, Society, and Performance* (1997), *Ayi Kwei Armah, Radical Iconoclast* (2000), and *Achebe and the Politics of Representation* (2001). His edited volume *The Life and Work of Frederick Douglass* is forthcoming from Duke University Press. He has contributed to a variety of books, including *The Cambridge History of African and Caribbean Literature* (2002), *The Foreign Woman in British Literature* (1999), *Postcolonial African Writers: A Bibliographical Sourcebook* (1998), and *Traditional Storytelling Today* (1999). Dr. Ogede's articles and reviews have appeared in major journals such as *Africa, African Affairs, African Literature Today, African Languages and Cultures, Africana Marburgensia, ARIEL: International Review of English Literature, Callaloo, International Fiction Review, International Folklore Review, Journal of African Cultural Studies, Lore and Language, Transition, Proverbium, Research in African Literatures, World Literature Today, Modern Fiction Studies, Kunapipi,* and *Matatu.*

DAVID D. PERLMUTTER completed his B.A. and M.A. at the University of Pennsylvania and his Ph.D. at the University of Minnesota. He is currently an associate professor at the Manship School of Mass Communication, Louisiana State University, as well as a senior fellow at the university's Reilly Center for Media and Public Affairs. Among his numerous publications are *Photojournalism and Foreign Policy* (1998), *The Manship School Guide to Political Communication* (1999), *Policing the Media* (2000), and *Visions of War* (2001). His published essays have also appeared in several journals, including *The Chronicle of Higher Education, Historical Methods, Visual Anthropology,* and *Journal of Communication.*

ROBERT SAMUELS teaches in the writing program at the University of California, Santa Barbara. He is the author of *Between Philosophy and Psychoanalysis* (1993), *Hitchcock's Bi-Textuality* (1998), and *Writing Prejudices* (2000). He is currently completing a book entitled *Teaching the e-Generation: The Effects of Computers and Popular Culture on College Writers.* He has published articles in a number of journals, including *JPCS: Journal for the Psychoanalysis of Culture, Clio's Psyche, Umbra, Studies in Psychoanalytic Theory, Strategies, Issues in Ego Psychology, N. P. A. P. News & Reviews,* and *The Newsletter of the Freudian Field.*

GLENN SHELDON received his Ph.D. in English from The University of Toledo, where he is currently assistant professor in the department of Interdisciplinary and Special Programs in University College. He teaches pre-composition writing classes and freshman-year experience classes as well as interdisciplinary seminars in Adult Liberal Studies Program which include "Latin American Art, Culture, and Literature" and "Food and Eating in U.S. Culture." He has published critical articles on the writing processes and modern American poetry. He is currently at work on an article entitled "Teaching Editing in the Writing Classroom."

DAVID STRONG has been chair of the Composition department at Winoma State University in Winoma, MN. Currently assistant professor of English at the University of Texas at Tyler, he received his Ph.D. with a specialization in Medieval and Renaissance British Literature as well composition pedagogy from Indiana University. In conjunction with courses on Chaucer and Shakespeare, he has taught a wide array of writing courses, including first-year composition, advanced expository writing, business writing, and basic skills. He has published extensively in the field of composition studies.

STEPHANIE VANDERSLICE is assistant professor of writing and the director of the Writing Project at the University of Central Arkansas. She holds an M.F.A. in fiction writing from George Mason University and a Ph.D. in English from the University of Louisiana at Lafayette. Her current research interests focus on undergraduate creative writing.

SANDRA VAVRA serves as assistant professor in the department of English at North Carolina Central University in Durham, North Carolina. In addition to managing the University Writing Lab, Professor Vavra teaches a variety of courses, including technical writing and advanced composition and secondary English methods. She received her Ph.D. in curriculum and instruction from the University of North Carolina at Chapel Hill. Her research interests focus on composition theory and pedagogy, academic service learning, vocabulary acquisition, and action research for in-service secondary teachers. She is currently developing a book on practical applications of service learning.